T0380529

DEFEAT THE LIONS AND BEARS BEFORE YOU HAVE TO FACE THE GOLIATHS

JIM ENNIS

WESTBOW
PRESS®
A DIVISION OF THOMAS NELSON
& ZONDERVAN

WestBow Press books may be ordered through booksellers or by contacting:

WestBow Press
A Division of Thomas Nelson & Zondervan
1663 Liberty Drive
Bloomington, IN 47403
www.westbowpress.com
844-714-3454

Scripture quotations marked KJV are taken from the King James Version.

ISBN: 979-8-3850-1815-4 (sc)
ISBN: 979-8-3850-1816-1 (hc)
ISBN: 979-8-3850-1814-7 (e)

Library of Congress Control Number: 2024902377

Print information available on the last page.

WestBow Press rev. date: 05/09/2024

CONTENTS

INTRODUCTION

And David said to Saul, Let no man's heart fail because of him; thy servant will go and fight with this Philistine. And Saul said to David, Thou art not able to go against this Philistine to fight with him: for thou art but a youth, and he a man of war from his youth. And David said unto Saul, Thy servant kept his father's sheep, and there came a lion, and a bear, and took a lamb out of the flock: And I went out after him, and smote him, and delivered it out of his mouth: and when he arose against me, I caught him by his beard, and smote him, and slew him. Thy servant slew both the lion and the bear: and this uncircumcised Philistine shall be as one of them, seeing he hath defied the armies of the living God. David said moreover, The Lord that delivered me out of the paw of the lion, and out of the paw of the bear, he will deliver me out of the hand of this Philistine. And Saul said unto David, Go, and the Lord be with thee. (1 Samuel 17:32–37)

David is primarily known for conquering Goliath; however, very little is said about the lion and bear that he fought while caring for his father's sheep. David learned from his battles and was not afraid to declare that the same God who gave him the power to defeat the lion and bear would also empower him to defeat Goliath.

This book addresses the LIONs, BEARs, and GOLIATHs we will face in our lives.

The lion and bear David fought represent internal conflicts, emotions, and feelings we face within ourselves during everyday life. In contrast, Goliath represents the external battles we will meet that are not part of our daily routine and may appear without much notice.

I pray that you will learn the characteristics of the lions and bears and be proficient in defeating them before you face the coming Goliaths.

Please indulge me in some areas:

1. The Bible speaks of only one bear, lion, and Goliath. The reader will need to accept some latitude that there may have been many battles with multiple lions and bears, but the information that David gave King Saul summarized all the conflicts David fought while tending his father's sheep.

2. The word *defeat* interchanges with *control* as we look at each aspect of the lions, bears, and Goliaths. Defeat does not always mean killing or destroying but may include setting a level of control or overcoming someone or something that once was a dominating factor.

    Please take your time reading this book. It may expose issues that will cause you to reflect on past and current battles. You may want to consider battles that lie ahead and the principles that the Lord has given us to be victorious over our faults and enemies.

This is your book. This is your time to reflect, analyze, and plan. Make notes and write your testimony in the provided spaces. Someday, someone may pick up your book and read your testimony, and in doing so, you may be the one who helps them overcome their LIONs and BEARs before they have to face their GOLIATHs.

BACKGROUND AND
PRINCIPLES

David, as is any child of God, was a complex being. He was chosen by God and known as a man after God's own heart (Acts 13:22), yet he was also human, had conflicts within himself, and sinned against the Lord several times. As a result, he paid high prices for his errors. However, David had the concept of repentance down to a science. He knew how to pray by expressing remorse for his sin, desiring to please the Lord, and ultimately, how to praise and get back to God.

No matter how far you stray from the Lord, it is not His will that you should perish but repent. Repent. Repent. Repent. He wants you to be successful. Remember, there is no such thing as success outside God's will, and there is no such thing as failure inside God's will. Being a millionaire does not necessarily describe success. What does it profit a man if he gains the whole world and loses his soul? (see Matthew 6:36) Nor does being poor describe a failure. For example, the angels were pallbearers for Lazarus, who was a beggar when he died (see Luke 16:22).

While David's brothers were away fighting the Philistines, David stayed behind to care for his father's sheep. Even though there was not a lot of glory or respect in being a shepherd, David learned skills that he unknowingly would be using when he faced Goliath. David learned to be *FAT*—faithful, available, and teachable. The scriptures are silent, but the possibilities are excellent that David learned a lot about himself and the power of God that would come upon him in time of need (Psalm 46:1), all the while going about his daily routine of taking care of his father's sheep.

Being a shepherd was considered by David's brothers to be a menial task while they were out fighting the Philistines, the work of real men, and they let him know where his place was when he showed up on the battlefield. (Today, it seems that everyone knows what everyone else should be doing, but they cannot fight their own battles.)

The honorable points we see in David at the beginning of this passage are that he was taking care of his father's sheep and being obedient to his father's directions.

In our walk with the Lord, we must learn to fight our shortcomings and the demonic forces we will encounter. Our first strategy should be to prioritize what is essential (Matthew 6:33). Above all else, we should desire to be in our Father's favor, with the ultimate objective being to hear Him say, well done, thou good and faithful servant: thou hast been faithful over a few things. I will make thee ruler over many things: enter thou into the joy of thy lord (see Matthew 25:21).

Our Lord's business and His will in our lives is powerful; we should start each morning by thanking Him for another day. He chose to wake you up and do something for Him. It wasn't the alarm clock, car horn, rooster, or anything else that woke you. The Lord allowed you to hear it, and this is the first sign that He has a plan for you—a blueprint for success that was drafted in the mind of God before your conception in your mother's womb.

The Lord also had a blueprint for Jeremiah before Jeremiah was conceived in his mother's womb (Jeremiah 1:5). In our daily routine, we must be mindful of the reason that we are here—our Father's business and His plan for us.

The first principle is that we must work for the Lord daily, show up and engage in our routines of family, life, and business while being aware of any change He may make to fulfill His will—which leads us to the second principle.

While David fed his father's sheep, Jesse called for him, and David answered. We should also listen for our Father's voice, but so often we are distracted by *our* routine that when the Lord is trying to speak to us, we are too involved to know.

A man was driving to a business appointment when he had a tire blowout, and his anxiety was already elevated. Now, he was concerned he would be late. The timing could not have been worse.

As he was changing the tire, a young man stopped and offered to help. The man, who did not disclose that he was a preacher, said, "Sure, I'll take all the help I can get," as he continued to think about his appointment and possibly being late.

While changing the tire, the young man told how he had backslid and strayed from God but was trying to get back to where he knew he should be. All the while, the preacher could only concentrate on getting the tire fixed and getting back on the road to his appointment. The young man continued to talk while they both changed the tire, which mostly annoyed the preacher, who was in a hurry.

After the tire was changed, the preacher thanked the young man and offered to pay him. The young man refused and expressed his willingness to be of assistance; however, he asked the preacher, still not knowing he was a preacher, to pray for him. The preacher acknowledged that he would, got into his car, and got back on the road to his appointment while never even asking the young man his name.

A few miles down the road, after realizing he would not be late for his appointment, the Lord spoke to the preacher. He'd had the blowout because God needed to send the young man to help him so the preacher would talk to him about God and help the young man. The preacher had to pull over because he wept so hard he could not see the road.

He prayed, "Lord, please forgive me. I was in such a hurry and worried about being late for my appointment that I didn't realize what was happening. Please send someone else to help him because I have failed you."

All too often, we get caught up in the distractions of life and lose focus on the fact that we are the servants of the Most High—and most of all, everything happens for a reason.

Prayer time: Lord, remind me daily that you order the steps of a good man and that I should not be consumed by the distractions and inconveniences that come my way. There *is* a reason for everything.

As we go forward, consider these two principles.

- I will be thankful every day and acknowledge that I am nothing on my own, and the Lord will direct my paths.

- My paycheck comes from (enter your boss's or company's name here), but I work for Jesus Christ. I am the servant of the Most High. Here am I, Lord; send me.

We have established those principles in our daily walk with the Lord. Let's be aware of the LIONs and BEARs that are ready to distract and attack us in our daily routines. These LIONs and BEARs are also our reactions to internal conflicts, emotions, and feelings due to our weaknesses. LIONs and BEARs do not come from the devil. They are already inside you, ready to roar whenever your weaknesses are under attack. For example, everyone has a temper. Some have mastered controlling it. In the worst scenarios, they stay cool, calm, and collected. But some have not. They get a hangnail and have a major meltdown. A car pulls out in front of them, and the rage is on. A waitress gets their order wrong, and it's the end of the world.

Since the LIONs and BEARs do not come from the devil, all the devil can do is influence you. He cannot make you do anything. We are free moral agents. Our actions are our choices, and our choices determine our destiny.

Similarly, God will not force you do anything, either. He can influence you, but the will to love and live for Him is yours and yours alone (Matthew 22:36–38; John 14:15).

Before we can discuss the GOLIATHs that we will face or the LAMBs (see Conclusion at the end of this book) that have been and will be placed in our care, we must first examine our hearts, minds, and souls. We will also learn about the strength and tools that God has given us to bring the LIONs and BEARs into subjection. The LIONs and BEARs are battles of self-control, and they will cause you to destroy more in a few seconds than you can build in years.

Let's look more closely at the characteristics of the LIONs and BEARs in our lives.

LIONs

If a man say, I love God, and hateth his brother, he is a liar: for he that loveth not his brother whom he hath seen, how can he love God whom he hath not seen? And this commandment have we from him, That he who loveth God love his brother also.

—1 JOHN 4:20–21

A new commandment I give unto you, That ye love one another; as I have loved you, that ye also love one another. By this shall all men know that ye are my disciples, if ye have love one to another.

—JOHN 13:34–35

LACK OF LOVE

There is a LION inside us just waiting to strike as soon as we are insulted, belittled, or emotionally attacked. It lies in waiting for the opportunity to destroy our love, compassion, charity, and any other emotion or feeling that we possess that helps us fulfill the second and great commandment given to us by Jesus Christ.

We will get to the first commandment a few chapters later, but let us look at the passage Mark recorded that contains the Lord's interaction with one of the scribes concerning the second commandment.

> And one of the scribes came, and having heard them reasoning together, and perceiving that he had answered them well, asked him, Which is the first commandment of all? And Jesus answered him, The first of all the commandments is, Hear, O Israel; The Lord our God is one Lord: And thou shalt love the Lord thy God with all thy heart, and with all thy soul, and with all thy mind, and with all thy strength: this is the

first commandment. And the second is like, namely this, Thou shalt love thy neighbor as thyself. There is none other commandment greater than these. (Mark 12:28–31)

One quality a child of God should possess and exhibit is love. John recorded that love is the identifier of being a disciple of Jesus Christ. Those are his words, not mine. Because they are living words, they expose flaws in our actions and words without love. Because love is the first and foremost characteristic of being a child of God, it also requires the most maintenance. This constant battle to keep our love topped off will make us cynical.

The constant bombardment of varying levels of hate by people who want to stretch our love to its limits will make this LION roar. While pointing out the deficiencies in our walk with Jesus Christ, these people claim to know what describes a person as a Christian. Many either do not know the Bible or only use scriptures as arguing points, not in their written context. It would be better if you discarded these distractions. And they are precisely that, distractions. These people are distractions. The chances are above average that the underlying reason they attack is that they have lost the battle to control their lack of love LION, and now you are seeing and feeling the results. They cannot contain their emotions, feelings, or rage any longer. Because of their lack of control, you have all the more reason not to give in and let the lack of love LION control your life. Look at them. Down deep, they are miserable. Beyond the sarcasm, cynical smiles, and mockery, their souls are hemorrhaging love, and soon they will no longer be identifiable as children of God. If they do not get their LION under control, they will end up losing the main component that makes them disciples of Jesus Christ, love.

Can you truly love someone if they do not return the love? No. Here is why. Love is cultivated by communication and interaction. Love does not just happen; it is more than words. It must undergo regular maintenance. If not, it dies. Our Lord said, "If you love me, keep my commandments." We know He loves us because He suffered and died for us, but what He said was the determining factor in telling us if we love Him. We must keep His commandments. So do you say you love Him or show it? Saying and showing are two different concepts, and I know from experience that words are wonderful to hear, but actions speak louder than words. The actions will prove whether or not the words are sincere.

If someone you love says, "I love you," and then slaps you on the cheek, our brains immediately go into self-examination mode. *Did I do something wrong? Did I say something that offended him or her? What just happened? Indeed, something must have happened that I missed.* The action does not fit the words. We will repeatedly defend the people we love, but after a while, if you keep kicking a dog, that dog will bite you. Sometimes a relationship will turn toxic and need to be severed, hopefully before all love is lost. Love is a two-way street; true love can only exist when love is returned.

Paul told the Galatians that the first characteristic of the fruit of the Spirit is love. During your daily routines, situations will arise that will affect your love, but remember, you must stay in control. Let nothing steal your love, because if you lose your love, you will lose your joy, your peace, and so on. This lack of love is detrimental to your walk with God and testimony.

As children of God, we are on display every day. Everything we do and say—our actions and reactions—is scrutinized under a microscope. Therefore, we must be in control of this LION. If we do not, we will say or do something that may damage the testimony of our walk with the Lord and hurt someone else in the process. In other words, the fruit of our Spirit begins to rot and stink, and if our fruit is rotten and stinking, how many people will we win to the Lord? You must control your lack of love LION to keep your fruit from damage.

Now that we have identified this LION, I wish we could kill it and never have to deal with it again. As we will see with the rest of the LIONs and BEARs, it cannot be destroyed, but it can be managed. Let's see why and how.

Why can we not kill this lack of love LION? We are human. As long as we are in these fleshly bodies, we will always have to contend with LIONs and BEARs. The Bible is filled with examples of struggles within us. Paul said he had to bring his body into subjection, and we must do the same. On a positive note on the inability to kill this LION, one side effect of the battles with the lack of love is that your prayer life will grow. These battles will cause us to look inward at our faults, repent, and ask the Lord for help controlling this LION. You cannot help how people treat you, but you control how you react. LIONs want you to react.

So how do we fight the lack of love LION? I wish it would be simple, but it probably will not be. Because situations change, so will the battles. Our problem is that many times we do not think before we react. When we do not stop, take a deep breath, and think, we usually blow up and say and do things that we cannot take back. Oh, the damage we caused because we reacted instead of keeping the LION under control. The Lord told us how to handle this LION: "Ye have heard that it hath been said, Thou shalt love thy neighbor, and hate thine enemy. But I say unto you, Love your enemies, bless them that curse you, do good to them that hate you, and pray for them which despitefully use you, and persecute you" (Matthew 5:43–44).

And now Paul's words:

> Bless them which persecute you: bless, and curse not. Recompense to no man evil for evil. Provide things honest in the sight of all men. If it be possible, as much as lieth in you, live peaceably with all men. Dearly beloved, avenge not yourselves, but rather give place unto wrath: for it is written, Vengeance is mine; I will repay, saith the Lord. Therefore if thine enemy hunger, feed him; if he thirst, give him drink: for in so doing thou shalt heap coals of fire on his head. Be not overcome of evil, but overcome evil with good. (Romans 12:14, 17–21)

What? That does not make sense and goes against everything that sounds normal! Well, you just read it. Their words, not mine. Bless them. Do good to them. Pray for them. Feed them, and give them something to drink. We do not want just to get even when we lose control of the LION. We want our enemies to hurt more than we hurt! If you broke one of my legs, I want to break both of your legs and an arm! As you read that, I know that down deep, you can identify. Why? Because we all came from the same flesh and have had similar feelings at some point and time when we were hurt. But if we keep the LION under control, we will obey the scriptures and be blessed in the long run.

Remember, the principle is not to let the battle cause you to react in a way that will destroy your love. The lack of love will also cause a wall to be built between you and the Lord. Your prayers will be hindered. Your focus will be blurred in your service to the Lord. Your lack of love will eventually hinder you. If you cannot control your temper, anger, and wrath, you will never be able to defeat the rest of the LIONs and BEARs, and you will be a pushover for the GOLIATHs headed your way.

Try this prayer: Lord, I cannot help how people treat me, but it still hurts. I need Your strength that took You through the hurt many gave you while You walked down here. This LION is screaming for me to give them a piece of my mind. Help me not to react so that I may retain my integrity with You through the battles. Thank You for Your promise that vengeance is Yours and that You will repay. I never want my prayers hindered or to find myself outside Your will. Please help me control this lack of love LION. In the name of Jesus Christ, amen.

INCONSISTENCY

"I know thy works, that thou art neither cold nor hot: I would thou wert cold or hot. So then because thou art lukewarm, and neither cold nor hot, I will spue thee out of my mouth" (Revelation 3:15–16).

God is looking for *FAT* people—*faithful, available, and teachable*—and inconsistency is the LION you will fight while obtaining these traits. When the Lord warned the Church in Laodicea about being lukewarm, He warned them about their inconsistency. Their focus on their works, their lusts, and their proud look became poison to them. This inconsistency is actually in all of us.

This Church, quite possibly a megachurch of its day, was rich in possessions. Today, it would be a focal point of the community full of committees, outreach programs, hunting clubs, fishing clubs, auxiliary clubs, singles clubs, ball teams, dance teams, choirs, and multimedia and social media programs. There would be enough resources to fund any program that might add to their attendance. With the abundance of materialistic things, anyone would classify them as blessed and in the will of God. But they were not.

How could it be possible to have the riches, status, and size of congregation that Laodicea had and still not be in God's favor? It starts at the top. When a pastor loses his vision, so goes the church. One might see this megachurch, with its vast array of activities and programs, and confirm these as signs of being in the will of God. We can, but the Lord does not. He looks for whether or not his children are consistent in their faithfulness to Him, available to follow His command, and capable of learning from their mistakes in their journey to hear Him say, "Well done."

It is so easy to get off course. It is so easy to become inconsistent. I have seen people who were consistent in attendance. They were at church services every time the doors were open, begin to miss one or two services, and before long, they quit attending church. The argument of the inconsistent is that the church will not save you. That is true to a point. However, if you do not maintain your vehicle, it will break down and possibly become irreparable. The church is God's maintenance plan that we must participate in for our spiritual well-being. Another argument of the inconsistent is that the church is full of hypocrites. This is also true to a point. However, well people do not go to the doctor or hospital. Those who do are sick, weak, and in need of help. This is what church is about—helping the sick and weak. We also have a biblical principle that God chooses the house of worship where he will dwell. In this place that He chooses—not us—to dwell, lives will be changed and the sick healed.

> If my people, which are called by my name,
> shall humble themselves, and pray, and

> seek my face, and turn from their wicked
> ways; then will I hear from heaven, and will
> forgive their sin, and will heal their land. Now
> mine eyes shall be open, and mine ears
> attent unto the prayer that is made in this
> place. For now have I chosen and sanctified
> this house, that my name may be there for
> ever: and mine eyes and mine heart shall
> be there perpetually. (2 Chronicles 7:14–16)

The only way God can be consistent with us is for us to be consistent with Him. The Bible is full of promises stating that if we do our part, God is faithful to do His part; however, He is not obligated to bless when we are inconsistent. "If ye be willing and obedient, ye shall eat the good of the land: But if ye refuse and rebel, ye shall be devoured with the sword: for the mouth of the LORD hath spoken it" (Isaiah 1:19–20).

When most people read the following scripture, all they see is money. Why? Because money has become their god. However, look at the overall context of the passage. "Bring ye all the tithes into the storehouse, that there may be meat in mine house, and prove me now herewith, saith the LORD of hosts, if I will not open you the windows of heaven, and pour you out a blessing, that there shall not be room enough to receive it" (Malachi 3:10).

The theme of this scripture is that God is saying, "Prove me." Try me. I double dare you to do your part and then watch me work. The problem is that many are unwilling to let go of *their* money. I stress *their* because it is not theirs to begin with; God is just allowing them to use it. We have many promises the Lord has made, yet many people cannot become consistent enough to reap the benefits. The inconsistent say, "I cannot afford to pay my tithes." The consistent and blessed say, "I cannot afford to not pay my tithes."

We have our ups and downs, days that we feel good and days that we feel bad; however, we must strive to be like Paul and learn to be content in whatsoever state we find ourselves. Fighting the LION of inconsistency is an ongoing process, just like the LION of lack of love. It is a fight to pray when we do not feel like our prayers even make it to the ceiling. It is a fight to fast when we do not have the drive to make the sacrifice of fasting that brings so much power to our walk with the Lord. It is a fight to do the right thing. But the more consistently we fight, the more strength we receive to fight.

The apostle James reminded the church that a double-minded man is unstable in all his ways (James 1:8). Being double-minded is a problem that produces inconsistency. But, as you read on, James tells them how to keep from being double-minded. "Submit yourselves therefore to God. Resist the devil, and he will flee from you. Draw nigh to God, and he will draw nigh to you. Cleanse your hands, ye sinners; and purify your hearts, ye double minded" (James 4:7–8).

Fixing inconsistency is simple yet challenging. Just follow the steps:

1. Submit;
2. Resist;
3. Draw nigh; and
4. Cleanse yourself.

Also, look at the promise embedded in step three. James said the Lord would draw nigh unto us. That promise is very much like 2 Chronicles 7:14: "If my people, which are called by my name, shall humble themselves, and pray, and seek my face, and turn from their wicked ways; then will I hear from heaven, and will forgive their sin, and will heal their land." This means, if we do our part, God will do His. *What a promise!* He will hear our prayer, forgive our sin, and heal our land. In other words, He will draw nigh unto us. But we have to do our part. He is not obligated to bless the unrighteous, and His promises are not for the inconsistent.

Consider this: you are blessed. Most people will acknowledge that they are blessed. Tell me something I do not know (he writes sarcastically). OK, here goes. You are blessed, but what blessings are you missing through inconsistency? I want to remind you that there is always room for improvement. Could you miss out on some blessings because you have reached a plateau in your walk with the Lord and assume you have made it to His perfect will? You might be selling yourself short and missing deeper depths and higher heights of blessings. Now, open your heart and mind and get consistent in doing what it takes to walk closer and draw nigh to Jesus Christ. Are you willing to take on the challenge? Many people will not take on the challenge to draw nigh because the more the Lord reveals the areas you need to change, the more you realize change is not easy. So how much do you want to be blessed? You know His promises are true, and He cannot lie. The ball is in your court.

There is also judgment for those who lose the fight to inconsistency. The Lord told the Laodiceans that he would spue them out of His mouth. Notice where the Laodiceans are located—in God's mouth. A place of power. A place of authority. It is through inconsistency that we become no threat to the devil. Our words are just a bunch of hot air. In other words, through inconsistency we lose all self-control. And when it comes time for us to speak to the GOLIATHs in our lives, they will not give us the time of day because we lost our authority and power when we lost the battle to the LION of inconsistency.

Try this prayer: Lord, I struggle with being consistent. I am distracted by so many things that I have to deal with daily (*name them*). It is hard to focus. Lord, please help me focus on You and take care of Your business. I believe strength, power, and authority will come if I can be more consistent in my walk with You. Please help me control this LION of inconsistency. In the name of Jesus Christ, amen.

OVERCOMING YOURSELF

"He that hath an ear, let him hear what the Spirit saith unto the churches; He that overcometh shall not be hurt of the second death" (Revelation 2:11).

Have you ever considered the biggest obstacle you must overcome in your walk with Jesus Christ? It is not the devil. It is not your wife or husband. It is not your family. It is not your job. Here is how to identify the biggest obstacle in your life. Go to the mirror. Look long and hard at what you see. See that person that looks like you? Talks like you? You have now identified your biggest obstacle. It is you.

We are our own worst enemy. We are human. We are born into sin. Our bodies, minds, and spirits *do not* want to do the things that please the Lord. For this reason, let us look at the first and greatest commandment.

> But when the Pharisees had heard that he had put the Sadducees to silence, they were gathered together. Then one of them, which was a lawyer, asked him a question, tempting him, and saying, Master, which is

the great commandment in the law? Jesus said unto him, Thou shalt love the Lord thy God with all thy heart, and with all thy soul, and with all thy mind. This is the first and great commandment. And the second is like unto it, Thou shalt love thy neighbor as thyself. On these two commandments hang all the law and the prophets. (Matthew 22:34–40)

If the first and greatest commandment is to love the Lord thy God with all thy heart, soul, and mind, then anything we put before God we make an idol. We can even make an idol of ourselves when we get the mentality that we can have it our way. In other words, my way or the highway. If you do not fight the LION of overcoming yourself and serve the Lord with all your heart, mind, soul, and strength, you have effectively placed your will above His. You are *not* His servant anymore. Your desires surpass His blessings. Your knowledge is greater than God's. Would anyone think this way? Some do adopt this mindset. However, some get very close to these thought processes by forgetting to pray. To ask for His will. To ask to be blessed. Things will start falling apart when we forget that Jesus Christ should be the Lord of our lives and when we do not make Him part of our daily routine. Situations may be that we have no choice but to fall on our knees in prayer.

I was in my office a few years ago working on daily tasks: making calls, sending emails, and running from room to room, overwhelmed by the number of things I needed to accomplish quickly. As I went down a hallway on the way to take care of another task, I turned a corner, and the Lord spoke to me. You will always remember the time, place, and situation if the Lord speaks to you.

He said, "Are you not going to speak to me today?"

It felt like the weight of the world came down on my shoulders, and I felt sorrow and hurt, as if I had just had a whipping from my dad. I felt the hurt and disappointment in His voice. I came to a screeching halt.

I said, "Lord, I never meant to not speak to You. I had so much on my mind this morning that I forgot. I am sorry and will do my best to speak to you as often as possible. Please forgive me."

I realized that if I am not consistent in talking to the Lord, His feelings get hurt, and it is easy to slowly slip into the mindset that He already knows my heart. I know my wife loves me, but it sure is nice to hear her say it! So much so that we should be telling the Lord how much He means to us. And in keeping the communication open, we fight and control the LION of overcoming ourselves.

Before any action is taken or the first word is said, battles are fought and won or lost inside us. We must make the conscious effort to live right, pray, ask for the Lord's will in our lives, and help overcome our selfish desires and lusts. This effort is not natural nor without plans, routines, and goals. For a child of God, the only defeats we should experience are those we allowed to happen because we lost the desire to fight the LION of overcoming ourselves. Paul said if God is for us, who can be against us? So defeat is not an option as long as we continue to fight to overcome our faults.

How do I overcome when bad things keep happening? First, bad things happen to good people. It rains on the just and unjust. Life happens. However, the children of God are constantly trying to look at the bigger picture and reminding themselves that no weapon formed against me shall prosper (see Isaiah 54:17) and all things work together for my good because I am the called according to His purpose (see Romans 8:28). Nothing can happen to me unless it goes across the Lord's desk first. He has to put His stamp of approval on everything before it can happen.

Somewhere deep inside the child of God, there is a warrior mentality that will come up from the dust saying, "Ye are of God, little children, and have overcome them: because greater is he that is in you than he that is in the world" (see 1 John 4:4).

I am more than a conqueror through Jesus Christ! He has already taken the stripes for my healing. Notice that He, being our example, overcame without sinning. You might say, "Well, He was God and had the power to overcome." He was God, but He was also flesh and felt pain and hunger, and He wept and bled like any other man.

> For we have not an high priest which cannot be touched with the feeling of our infirmities; but was in all points tempted like as we are, yet without sin. Let us therefore come boldly unto the throne of grace, that we may obtain mercy, and find grace to help in time of need. (Hebrews 4:15–16)

Reread verse 16. "Let us therefore come boldly unto the throne of grace, that we may obtain mercy, and find grace to help in time of need." (see Hebrews

4:16) We have a recipe that will help us overcome. Quit whimpering, and come boldly to the throne of grace. Get involved in your prayer. Show some fortitude and excitement.

I get excited just thinking about the promises of what He can do, whether He does it or not. I have lived for the Lord long enough to have seen a few miracles. So I not only believe, I know, that with God, all things are possible. I have gotten to see some things that would make many people shake their heads in disbelief. I do not just believe; I know. If you follow me with that statement, you understand that the word *believe* hints at having not seen or proven something. However, when you *know* something to be a fact, you have more than likely proven it, seen it happen, or had it happen to you. It is one thing to *believe* that God can heal, but when it happens to you, from now on, you *know* God is the Healer!

Why do we come before the Lord with boldness? The squeaky wheel gets the grease! Just ask the centurion:

> And when Jesus was entered into Capernaum, there came unto him a centurion, beseeching him, And saying, Lord, my servant lieth at home sick of the palsy, grievously tormented. And Jesus saith unto him, I will come and heal him. The centurion answered and said, Lord, I am not worthy that thou shouldest come under my roof: but speak the word only, and my servant shall be healed. For I am a man under authority, having soldiers under me: and I say to this man, Go, and he goeth; and

to another, Come, and he cometh; and to my servant, Do this, and he doeth it. When Jesus heard it, he marveled, and said to them that followed, Verily I say unto you, I have not found so great faith, no, not in Israel. (Matthew 8:5–10)

Or, ask the woman from Canaan:

And, behold, a woman of Canaan came out of the same coasts, and cried unto him, saying, Have mercy on me, O Lord, thou Son of David; my daughter is grievously vexed with a devil. But he answered her not a word. And his disciples came and besought him, saying, Send her away; for she crieth after us. But he answered and said, I am not sent but unto the lost sheep of the house of Israel. Then came she and worshipped him, saying, Lord, help me. But he answered and said, It is not meet to take the children's bread, and to cast it to dogs. And she said, Truth, Lord: yet the dogs eat of the crumbs which fall from their masters' table. Then Jesus answered and said unto her, O woman, great is thy faith: be it unto thee even as thou wilt. And her daughter was made whole from that very hour. (Matthew 15:22–28)

Boldness gets God's attention. Boldness gets results. If you need help fighting the LION of overcoming yourself, it may be time to take a bolder approach and get some heavenly help.

The Lord also uses situations to get us to pause, refocus, repent, and then move forward. Consider this when remembering that nothing can happen unless it gets Jesus Christ's stamp of approval, for He is the Almighty God. "As many as I love, I rebuke and chasten: be zealous therefore, and repent" (Revelation 3:19).

Instead of focusing on the hurt and pain of correction, focus on the fact that if the Lord did not love you, He would not chastise you. Be zealous. Be bold. Thank Him for loving you. *And repent!*

A weapon to help you in your battle: "And they overcame him by the blood of the Lamb, and by the word of their testimony; and they loved not their lives unto the death" (Revelation 12:11).

Your testimony will help you fight the LION of overcoming yourself. If you speak defeat, you will be defeated. If you speak victory, you shall overcome. Find the scriptures that speak victory. Learn them. Quote them. Say them out loud. You need to hear yourself speaking victoriously. Remember, there is power and authority in your words. Or is it in the Word of God … or both?

Remember, the LION of overcoming yourself is a fight that only you can fight. I can pray with you and put you on every prayer list in the world, but the fight is yours at the end of the day. The child of God will also remember that, "I can do all things through Christ which strengtheneth me." (see Philippians 4:13) We are only failures once we decide to quit.

Try this prayer. Lord, I have a lot of baggage. I get my priorities (*name them*) out of line a lot. The things that I feel are important many times are not. I have gotten out of your will and service to get more stuff, but your word says to seek your kingdom and your righteousness first, and all the stuff will come later. Thank you for loving me, especially when I forget to show my love for you. Please help me control this LION of overcoming myself. In the name of Jesus Christ, amen.

NEGATIVITY

"Do all things without murmurings and disputings: That ye may be blameless and harmless, the sons of God, without rebuke, in the midst of a crooked and perverse nation, among whom ye shine as lights in the world" (Philippians 2:14–15).

"Let no corrupt communication proceed out of your mouth, but that which is good to the use of edifying, that it may minister grace unto the hearers. And grieve not the holy Spirit of God, whereby ye are sealed unto the day of redemption" (Ephesians 4:29–30).

One of the most destructive spirits that wants to raise its head within us is the LION of negativity. It can be likened to cancer: all it takes is one cell to become deformed. Then it begins to multiply, attach itself to healthy tissue, and slowly consumes the whole body. The LION starts the battle with a bad situation. The situations usually come from something that catches you off guard or has gone on for so long that you do not expect to see any change for the good.

If you do not get the LION under control immediately, the LION will turn the negative into depression and then into despair. If you have ever been around someone in despair, they are pitiful. There is very little that you can say or do for them. The LION of negativity has done so much damage that many people see no way of ever getting better. This LION can take a perfectly delightful and healthy person and make him or her suicidal. This is not God's will, and if you or someone you know is at this level of despair, get help for yourself or them *now*.

Stopping negativity is one of the top priorities of supervisors. Millions, if not billions, of dollars are spent each year on motivational speaking and promoting positive thinking. People are more productive when the atmosphere is positive. Who does not like to feel good? Who does not want to walk away from a conversation feeling better than when you started? There are people out there who are miserable and want you to be miserable. Things are bad and getting worse by the minute. Doom and gloom. If it were not for bad luck, they would have no luck at all. If they won the lottery (which I recommend against playing), they would gripe because they would have to pay so much in taxes.

A depressed man was drinking coffee with a friend one day. He was telling his friend how bad his life was and that he had so few friends that the funeral home would have to hire pallbearers for his funeral.

With the hope that shock might help, the friend said, "Nope. They won't have to hire pallbearers for you. I know six guys who will gladly step up to make sure you get to the grave."

Here is the wisdom of Solomon: "A merry heart doeth good like a medicine: but a broken spirit drieth the bones" (Proverbs 17:22).

One of the greatest weapons we can use to fight the LION of negativity is laughter. I believe a merry heart gets the blood flowing and eventually filters out negativity, depression, and despair. I have made funeral arrangements with families that were joyful meetings. After the arrangement meeting was over, some staff would come to me saying they could hear us laughing from their office with the door closed. How is it possible to take the death of a loved one and turn it into a joyous occasion?

Many times they use the excuse of being a realist. Sometimes they are right. They are... wait for it... in all reality, negative. The choice is ours. We decide if we want to dwell on the reality of the negative or the reality of the positive.

The LION of negativity loves to roar its "realistic" views of situations: I hate my job. My supervisor is an idiot. My wife complains all the time. My children are spoiled and entitled. My husband is lazy. Our church services are dead. The pastor has his picks in the church. I could go on and on about the negativity I have heard over the years. There have been times that I have had to excuse myself from a conversation because I could feel the LION of negativity affecting me! How miserable! I do not want to be around these people unless I can help them. But most of the time, it is hard to help someone battle this LION.

In the south, my area of the country, we have a vine called kudzu. It is an aggressive plant that will cover the ground and kill anything, including trees, that it grows over. Its coverage is so dense that it blocks all sunlight. The only way to stop kudzu is to kill the root.

Just as the kudzu is so aggressive and deadly to the vegetation it covers, so is the LION of negativity. If you do not kill the root of negativity, it will begin to cover every aspect of your life. It will take control of your job, family, and church and eventually destroy your walk with God.

Before the root can start, a seed must be planted. Not only do we have to keep the negative winds of gossip and hearsay from blowing seeds into our souls, we have to keep checking our conversation so we are not also sowing discord. The more you hang around negative people, the more negative you become.

Of all of the conversations that will promote the growth of negativity, the greatest is complaining. Complaining cost the Hebrews forty years of wandering in the wilderness after they came out of Egypt. Complaining kept everyone over age twenty-five, except for Joshua and Caleb, from getting into the Promised Land. Guess what? Complaining makes God mad. And you will not like it when He gets angry. Complaining builds a wall between the Lord and us, and our blessings are gradually cut off. How does this work? When you complain to your wife, husband, or friend, how long does it take before the relationship becomes troubled?

The same thing happens when we complain, and the Lord hears it. "For God hath not given us the spirit of fear; but of power, and of love, and of a sound mind" (2 Timothy 1:7).

A tool that the LION of negativity uses is fear, and a powerful tool it is. It will take reasonably strong children of God who have seen God's power and turn them into whining, blabbering mental cases. It will cause them to forget the promises in the scriptures and eventually turn their backs on God. Children learn from the environment they live. If they are told day in and day out that they are worthless, they will have low self-esteem and consider themselves failures. We also are products of our environment. If we cultivate negativity, everything will always be bad and getting worse. If we learn to praise God, negativity is defeated.

How do you keep a guard on the LION of negativity?

"That ye put off concerning the former conversation the old man, which is corrupt according to the deceitful lusts; And be renewed in the spirit of your mind; And that ye put on the new man, which after God is created in righteousness and true holiness" (Ephesians 4:22–24).

First, think about what you say before you say it! Is what you are getting ready to say going to build up or tear down? Do the people I hang around with cultivate my negativity?

Second, you must learn how to worship. Worship is not something you do only on Sunday mornings, Sunday nights, or Wednesday nights. Worship is a lifestyle that includes minor things like praying over your meal and talking to your wife, husband, or friend about how you are blessed. You have to learn ways to retain God in your knowledge continually. As Paul said, pray without ceasing. Does that mean we have to be on our knees 24/7? Absolutely not. But we can have a prayer on our lips and in our hearts and minds. The more you keep the Lord on your mind and the abundance of blessings he has bestowed on you, the less time you will feed the LION of negativity.

Try this prayer. Lord, the battle of fighting the LION of negativity is hard, so hard that sometimes I want to throw up my hands and quit. I know this is not Your will. Help me find joy and create a merry heart when the battle is relentless. I know it is not Your will for me to be negative, depressed, or in a state of despair. I can do all things through You who strengthens me. In the name of Jesus Christ, amen.

BEARs

Pride goeth before destruction, and an haughty spirit before a fall.

—PROVERBS 16:18

This know also, that in the last days perilous times shall come. For men shall be lovers of their own selves.

2 TIMOTHY 3:1–2

BOASTING

One of the works of the flesh is idolatry. Many people will automatically associate a large sculpture or statue with being an idol. However, worshipping or praying to statues and sculptures is not the only form of idolatry. Idolatry can be painted with a broad stroke to encompass several scenarios. Idolatry is simply anything that you place before your walk with God. Jesus Christ is the head of our life, or He is not. He does not play second fiddle to anyone or anything.

The apostle James sums it up by saying that if we know to do good and do it not, it is sin (see James 4:17). By association, if we see that it is wrong and do it, it is also sin. But remember, the choice is ours alone. Letting our conscience be our guide is not scriptural. Simply put, we can make ourselves an idol through self-righteousness. You might ask, how can I make myself my idol? It might be easier than you think. You may already, unknowingly, have some of the characteristics. Once a fault is revealed, your future, both in this life and in eternity, will be determined by what you do with that knowledge.

Let us look at the self-righteousness BEAR of boasting from the story Luke recorded about the rich man.

> And he spake a parable unto them, saying,
> The ground of a certain rich man brought
> forth plentifully: And he thought within
> himself, saying, What shall I do, because
> I have no room where to bestow my fruits?
> And he said, This will I do: I will pull down
> my barns, and build greater; and there will
> I bestow all my fruits and my goods. And I
> will say to my soul, Soul, thou hast much
> goods laid up for many years; take thine
> ease, eat, drink, and be merry. But God said
> unto him, Thou fool, this night thy soul shall
> be required of thee: then whose shall those
> things be, which thou hast provided? So is
> he that layeth up treasure for himself, and is
> not rich toward God. (Luke 12:16–21)

The rich man had an abundant harvest. He was blessed. Next, he thought within himself about what to do with the bountiful amount of fruit. He should have given thanks to the Lord first, since from the Lord is where all blessings flow, but he did not. His verbiage concerning possession used only *I* and *my*. It never contained any context of God. Then he made plans without consulting the Lord's will.

Everything we have is because the Lord has seen fit to share it with us. We do not own one single thing. Just because there is a piece of paper that says your house or car belongs to you does not mean you have complete ownership. It has been loaned to you by the Lord, and He leaves it up to you to be a good steward of it.

There is absolutely nothing wrong with making plans and having goals. The problem we run into is when ours are different from the Lord's plans and goals for us. All people are born with a blueprint for their lives. The Lord had one for Jeremiah (see Jeremiah 1:4-5), and He has one for you too.

Our trouble starts when we listen to the BEAR of boasting. We listen and then act on our desires, plans, and goals. You will always fall when you are outside the Lord's will. You may wonder, *Why do so many people seem to be blessed while I struggle?* This study is not about them. It is about you listening to the BEAR of boasting instead of listening to and following the Lord.

The rich man then turns it up by taking charge of his soul. The word for soul here can be translated as *breath* or *spirit*, but it also has ties to words that can be translated as *heart, mind,* and *soul.* The Lord said the greatest commandment is to love the Lord thy God with all thy heart, mind, and soul. When the rich man addressed his soul, he, in a sense, had begun to love himself above the Lord, and this will never end well. This is nothing less than the BEAR of boasting speaking, which is idolatry, and the BEAR is about to get the rich man destroyed.

How does the Lord look at his children who boast, refuse to be thankful, and become self-righteous? Just as He did the rich man, God calls them fools. Notice that this is a "but God" moment. Many will use the phrase "but God" to say that your struggles, issues, and failures are just a transition in the process of the Lord getting ready to bless you. Not in this case. The "but God" here is a transition, but not in a positive way. It is a transition of His coming judgment.

Thou fool. Say it out loud, and let it ring in your ears. Thou fool. Will God call you a fool? He will if you do not keep the BEAR of boasting under control. It is already inside you, but you have to control it.

As a result of the rich man boasting, the Lord said his soul would be required of him. The original word for *required* is also translated as *demand back*. Since we know the word soul is also translated as *breath*, in essence, the Lord told the rich man, "I will take your breath back." When God breathed life into Adam, He made him a living soul. When we die, the Lord takes back His breath/ soul. After all, our breath/soul is not ours. Everything belongs to God. We see that the rich man's supposed ownership of his soul was not a valid statement. Do not let the BEAR of boasting cause the Lord to call you a fool and lose your soul.

"The wicked shall be turned into hell, and all the nations that forget God" (Psalm 9:17). Plentiful are the warnings against the BEAR of boasting throughout the Bible.

"Trust in the LORD with all thine heart; and lean not unto thine own understanding. In all thy ways acknowledge him, and he shall direct thy paths. Be not wise in thine own eyes: fear the LORD, and depart from evil. It shall be health to thy navel, and marrow to thy bones" (Proverbs 3:5–8).

> For thou hast trusted in thy wickedness: thou hast said, None seeth me. Thy wisdom and thy knowledge, it hath perverted thee; and thou hast said in thine heart, I am, and none else beside me. Therefore shall evil

> come upon thee; thou shalt not know from
> whence it riseth: and mischief shall fall upon
> thee; thou shalt not be able to put it off: and
> desolation shall come upon thee suddenly,
> which thou shalt not know. (Isaiah 47:10–11)

"Professing themselves to be wise, they became fools" (Romans 1:22).

"And even as they did not like to retain God in their knowledge, God gave them over to a reprobate mind, to do those things which are not convenient" (Romans 1:28).

James gives us the strategy for controlling this BEAR:

> Go to now, ye that say, To day or to morrow
> we will go into such a city, and continue
> there a year, and buy and sell, and get
> gain: Whereas ye know not what shall be
> on the morrow. For what is your life? It is
> even a vapor, that appeareth for a little
> time, and then vanisheth away. For that ye
> ought to say, If the Lord will, we shall live,
> and do this, or that. But now ye rejoice in
> your boastings: all such rejoicing is evil.
> Therefore to him that knoweth to do good,
> and doeth it not, to him it is sin. (James
> 4:13–17)

James says many people are goal-oriented to the point that they have all their plans made and have accounted for almost every possibility of making everything come together to meet their goals. However, there is one factor that almost everyone discounts. You do not know what tomorrow may bring. You plan for the next ten, twenty, thirty, forty, or fifty years, but you do not know if you will live to see the sunrise in the morning. A saying that many of our elders used has faded over time. They understood James's directive and adapted it to any plans they may have made, ending it with "if the good Lord is willing and the creek don't rise."

Why do we not still say, "Lord willing," today? Society has changed, and the children of God are adapting to it. We are hesitant to say much concerning our walk with God. But we should still be saying, "Lord willing," because as servants of the Most High, our plans should be flexible and our goals changeable because we are His servants. He is *not* our servant.

James says in the verse that you boast in your self-confidence or pride, and all such boasting is evil. *Wow!* Why would it be evil? You have allowed the BEAR of boasting to speak, and God could very well call you a fool if you do not ask for and include Him in your plans and goals. If you do not, it is sin, and no sin shall enter heaven. That is a tough pill to swallow, but it is plain and simple. Either Jesus Christ is the Lord of your life, or He is not. It is your choice to let Him be your pilot or not. He is no one's copilot. Ever.

Another weapon that we can use against the BEAR of boasting is humility. Peter has solid advice on the effects of humility.

> All of you be subject one to another, and
> be clothed with humility: for God resisteth
> the proud, and giveth grace to the humble.
> Humble yourselves therefore under the

mighty hand of God, that he may exalt you
in due time: Casting all your care upon him;
for he careth for you. (1 Peter 5:5–7)

Consider this. Clothing is for protection from the elements and often for retaining body heat. If you are clothed with humility, you have a strong barrier between you and the elements and containment of things inside you that do not need to get out. You also get to choose the thickness of your clothing (humility). The stronger your clothing (humility), the more contained you keep the BEAR! It would be great if we could make humility as strong as titanium or stronger! The clothing of humility may very well be the key to keeping the LIONs and BEARs contained!

Try this prayer: Lord, thank you for exposing the LIONs and BEARs in my life. It is so easy to boast and not even realize it. Show me. Correct me. Help me to keep my boasting under control. Sometimes my ego gets the best of me. I know that I am nothing and have nothing without you. Help me to be clothed in humility. Help me to make it bulletproof and strong enough to keep the LIONs and BEARs contained. Thank you in advance for being a very present help in the time of need. In the name of Jesus Christ. Amen.

ENVY

"Let not thine heart envy sinners: but be thou in the fear of the LORD all the day long" (Proverbs 23:17).

We are going to look at the word envy and some similar words. Envy can also appear in words like jealousy and covetousness. Let us break these words down and then see what they have in common. The BEAR of envy says, "I like what you have. I want it too." Jealousy will say, "I want what you have, and until I get it, you cannot have it either." Covetousness will say, "I want what you have." To ease understanding of this BEAR, we will combine jealousy and covetousness with the word envy and define it as desiring something we do not have in our possession.

In the story of Cain and Abel, we find Cain envious of Abel's sacrifice to the Lord.

> And in process of time it came to pass, that Cain brought of the fruit of the ground an offering unto the LORD. And Abel, he also brought of the firstlings of his flock and of the fat thereof. And the LORD had respect

unto Abel and to his offering: But unto Cain
and to his offering he had not respect. And
Cain was very wroth, and his countenance
fell. (Genesis 4:3–5)

First, notice the differences in the offerings. Cain
brought the fruit of the ground. Abel brought the firstlings
and the fat. Cain gave the Lord the scraps and kept the
best. In contrast, Abel offered the firstlings, the best, and
the fat, which was highly valuable in its usage in many
applications. In other words, Abel made the true sacrifice,
and Cain gave the Lord what he did not want to keep or
sell (the leftovers).

The book of Hebrews confirms that God accepted
Abel's sacrifice and called him righteous. "By faith Abel
offered unto God a more excellent sacrifice than Cain, by
which he obtained witness that he was righteous, God
testifying of his gifts" (Hebrews 11:4).

Second, notice that the Lord respected Abel's offering
but not Cain's. But, someone might say, "I thought the
Bible says God is not a respecter of persons." It does.
God does not respect people, but He does our actions.
Consider this. Most parents love their children the same.
However, parents are closer to some children than others.
Why? It is often because their relationship is deeper with
certain children. They live closer, visit more often, or their
personalities click. They love their children the same,
but the closeness is much more solid because love is
returned.

Our relationship with the Lord is similar. He loves us
the same, but when we choose to draw nigh unto Him, He
keeps His promise in drawing nigh to us. As a result, our

relationship with the Lord will be much deeper. The closer we walk with Him, the greater the peace that passes all understanding. The more we acknowledge His blessings, the more blessings we receive.

Two people each give you a gift. One brings their gift to you, looks you in the eye and congratulates or thanks you, places the gift in your hands, and maybe hugs you. The gift is wrapped in beautiful paper and a big bow, with a thoughtful card attached, and when you open it, it is like that person read your mind. The gift is what you always wanted! It is perfect!

The other person brings a gift to you. As this person approach you, the body language and facial expression scream that he or she would rather be anywhere but there. The gift is in a plastic bag from the store. The bag is pitched to you, the gift-giver says, "It ain't much," and turns and walks away without breaking stride.

You look into the bag and realize the gift-giver was telling the truth: "It ain't much." It took no more than five minutes to pick out the gift. No thought. No intent other than this person *had* to get you a gift.

Given that scenario, which gift would you want to receive? More importantly, which person do you want giving the gift? As we live for the Lord, we are either the cheerful giver that the scripture tells about, or we are Cain.

Our closeness to or distance from the Lord, the abundance or lack of blessings, is a direct result of *our* choices, not His. He is not slack concerning His promises. Here's another promise that is closely connected. "Blessed are they which do hunger and thirst after righteousness: for they shall be filled" (Matthew 5:6).

You grow cold and distant in your relationship with the Lord because either you aren't hungry, or you are hungry for the wrong things. Your priorities are outside His will, and as long as you are not in His will, you will always fight losing battles against the LIONs and BEARs.

Cain got mad and pouted because he wanted the same recognition as Abel while giving the Lord the scraps. Be prepared if you only want to live your life the way you want. The BEAR of envy will be a challenging and continuous battle. "Jealousy is cruel as the grave: the coals thereof are coals of fire, which hath a most vehement flame" (Song of Solomon 8:6).

Solomon said jealousy would destroy you. Guess where jealousy's fire burns—inside you. Guess where the BEAR of envy is. Also inside. It is indeed an internal battle that only we can control. The good news is Jesus Christ is alive and well and willing to help us in our infirmities and battles, but only if we ask.

More good news comes from Paul. He tells us of things we *should* covet.

> And God hath set some in the church, first apostles, secondarily prophets, thirdly teachers, after that miracles, then gifts of healings, helps, governments, diversities of tongues. Are all apostles? are all prophets? are all teachers? are all workers of miracles? Have all the gifts of healing? do all speak with tongues? do all interpret? But covet earnestly the best gifts: and yet shew I unto you a more excellent way. (1 Corinthians 12:28–30)

Paul begins by telling us that there are callings that God has set in the church. He then clarifies that not everyone has the same calling because this would be counterproductive and cause confusion. Paul ends this chapter by saying it is good, right, and proper to desire the best gifts and to be used in the service of Jesus Christ. Paul continues in the next chapter, showing the "more excellent way." He says that with all the gifts, callings, and ways that we may be used in the service of the Lord, if we do not have love, the things we do mean very little.

The BEAR of envy does not want you to covet the gift of the Holy Ghost nor the gifts of the Spirit. It only wants you to be envious, jealous, and covetous of the things of this world.

> Love not the world, neither the things that are in the world. If any man love the world, the love of the Father is not in him. For all that is in the world, the lust of the flesh, and the lust of the eyes, and the pride of life, is not of the Father, but is of the world. And the world passeth away, and the lust thereof: but he that doeth the will of God abideth for ever. (1 John 2:15–17)

The BEAR of envy will cause you to do things you would not normally do. Lust, if not controlled, turns into envy, jealousy, and covetousness, which will cause many heartaches. The BEAR of envy will take that lust and put you into debt while trying to buy happiness. It will turn a perfect marriage into a divorce. It will cause a person who drinks occasionally to become an alcoholic.

It will cause a person who dabbled in drugs to become addicted and lose everything. The BEAR knows how to attack our weaknesses, but controlling the BEAR is our job. Thankfully, we have hope and help in Jesus Christ.

So how do we fight the BEAR of envy? If you want to control your BEAR of envy, you take away its food. The BEAR feeds on lust. You must have self-control over your weaknesses. But how?

> Is any among you afflicted? let him pray.
> Is any merry? let him sing psalms. Is any
> sick among you? let him call for the elders
> of the church; and let them pray over him,
> anointing him with oil in the name of the
> Lord: And the prayer of faith shall save the
> sick, and the Lord shall raise him up; and
> if he have committed sins, they shall be
> forgiven him. Confess your faults one to
> another, and pray one for another, that ye
> may be healed. The effectual fervent prayer
> of a righteous man availeth much. (James
> 5:13–16)

Once you admit to yourself and Jesus Christ that you have a problem, you can start making progress. Next, start pouring your heart out in prayer and asking the Lord for help. Then, you need a prayer partner. A person of confidence. A kindred spirit. A person you can trust implicitly. James said for us to call for the elders of the church. These were not only men who held the office of elder but those who had proven themselves to be wise and filled with the Holy Ghost. Pillars of faith, like the elders, can be one of your greatest weapons in the fight against the BEAR of envy.

The next thing James said to do was something that is gradually being lost in churches today. James said for us to anoint with oil in the name of the Lord. Some might say, "I will never have oil poured on my head!," "It will mess up my hair," or "That's why we have doctors."

My response would be, "OK. This is not a commandment. But if you want to be healed of natural sicknesses, mental illness, or spiritual issues, you might want to consider trying what the Bible recommends."

The Word of God is tried and proven. All you need is faith to believe. That's what James said, the prayer of faith will save the sick. As I have stated before, I not only believe God is a healer, I know He is. I have not only seen it happen, I have been healed.

Warning! Be careful to whom you confess your faults. Not everyone is honest and may blackmail you. You need—must have—a prayer partner. Remember what the Lord said: "Again I say unto you, That if two of you shall agree on earth as touching any thing that they shall ask, it shall be done for them of my Father which is in heaven. For where two or three are gathered together in my name, there am I in the midst of them" (Matthew 18:19–20).

These are His words and promise. Watch out! The BEAR of envy does not like prayer partners. Prayer partners make it vulnerable, and the BEAR does not want to be defeated.

Lastly, notice the type of prayer that we should pray. "The effectual fervent prayer of a righteous man availeth much." (see James 5:16) Not a wimpy repetition of words, but an outpouring petition from your prayer closet, causing heaven to stand at attention! So fervent that you can feel the hair stand up on your neck! But notice this clarifier on the one doing the praying. A prayer that will cause the angels to listen and the demons to run for cover will come from a righteous person.

Simply put, a righteous person begins just by trying to do the right things (things that please the Lord), and then the more right things he or she does, the more righteous that person becomes. The more righteous, the holier as well. That is when you reach the level where the angels pay attention to you, and the demons run because of the power and authority that comes from you.

The more righteous you become and the more fervent your prayers, the more the BEAR of envy starts listening to you instead of you listening to the BEAR! Praise God!

Try this prayer: Lord, I am tired of being controlled by the BEAR of envy. I am learning to be content and a good steward of what You have given me. Please help me fight this BEAR. Please help my prayers become more fervent and my walk with You more righteous. I need the power and authority to keep the LIONS and BEARS under control. In the name of Jesus Christ, amen.

ADDICTIONS

"Wherefore seeing we also are compassed about with so great a cloud of witnesses, let us lay aside every weight, and the sin which doth so easily beset us, and let us run with patience the race that is set before us" (Hebrews 12:1).

No matter the size of the BEAR of addictions, it is still a BEAR.

Society plays a big part in determining and classifying what is considered acceptable addictions and what is considered the most heinous and despicable addictions. Even though the Bible is where most of our laws are derived from, please remember that God looks at many things from a far different perspective than we do. Just because society has deemed it appropriate or acceptable, in this current world in which we live, it probably is neither appropriate nor acceptable in the eyes of God.

The BEAR of addictions is one of the most controlling BEARS. It may consume every waking moment. It knows the things that tempt you. It must be fed and will keep you awake until it is fed. Whether your addiction is private or public, it haunts you. You cannot shake it. Everywhere you look, you see your addiction. The BEAR of addiction is always on the job, and that job is to consume your heart, mind, soul, and strength.

Where does the BEAR of addiction come from? You might be surprised to know it may be hereditary. At least, hereditary would be the scientific word that is appropriate in our culture.

The Bible calls it something else. "The LORD is longsuffering, and of great mercy, forgiving iniquity and transgression, and by no means clearing the guilty, visiting the iniquity of the fathers upon the children unto the third and fourth generation" (Numbers 14:18).

In several places, the Bible records that the sins of our forefathers will carry over from generation to generation. We call it a generational curse. Let me also pair this thought with scripture on raising children. "Train up a child in the way he should go: and when he is old, he will not depart from it" (Proverbs 22:6).

This scripture has both good and bad implications. The good implications are that if you train children to live for God with all of their hearts, minds, souls, and strength, they will not depart from it.

This scripture can also have bad implications because a generational curse can follow from the sins committed by their parents. For example, if a parent prays openly and also with the child, more than likely the child will learn to pray on own his or her own. In like manner, if a son sees his father beat up his mother, he learns it is appropriate for him to beat his wife when he gets married. If the daughter sees her father beat her mother, she will think it is normal for her husband to beat her. Another example is if a daughter sees her mother being unfaithful and hiding things or information from her husband (the daughter's father), would you like to guess what behavior the daughter will exhibit when she gets married? I have seen this happen over three generations. If a son sees his father taking what does not belong to him, would you like to guess what the son will grow up to be? If you said a thief, you are 100 percent correct.

Children live what they learn, and we either train them in the ways of the Lord or the ways of the world. If there are generational curses, could there be generational blessings? Let's see.

> Josiah was eight years old when he began to reign, and he reigned thirty and one years in Jerusalem. And his mother's name was Jedidah, the daughter of Adaiah of Boscath. And he did that which was right in the sight of the LORD, and walked in all the way of David, his father, and turned not aside to the right hand or to the left. (2 Kings 22:1–2)

> And the LORD was with Jehoshaphat, because he walked in the first ways of his father David, and sought not unto Baalim; But sought to the LORD God of his father, and walked in his commandments, and not after the doings of Israel. Therefore the LORD stablished the kingdom in his hand; and all Judah brought to Jehoshaphat presents; and he had riches and honor in abundance. (2 Chronicles 17:3–5)

Here we have examples of sons blessed because they followed the Lord like their fathers. But every generation has a choice—breaking the curse or being ruled by the BEAR of addiction. Are you training your children and grandchildren in the ways of the Lord, or are you setting the standards of this world as the important things in life? *You* set the standard. *You* are cursing or blessing your children. When they become adults, what will they carry to their children, blessings or curses?

> I call heaven and earth to record this day against you, that I have set before you life and death, blessing and cursing: therefore choose life, that both thou and thy seed may live: That thou mayest love the LORD thy God, and that thou mayest obey his voice, and that thou mayest cleave unto him: for he is thy life, and the length of thy days: that thou mayest dwell in the land which the LORD sware unto thy fathers, to Abraham, to Isaac, and to Jacob, to give them. (Deuteronomy 30:19–20)

Some say science has proven that addictions are chemical imbalances that can be treated but not stopped. Science says a bumblebee cannot fly. I guess the bumblebee missed that class. Our scientific conclusions do not bind God. Before Sir Isaac Newton stated the law of gravity, it already existed because God created it.

I believe and know that many things are not possible with men, but with God, *all* things are possible. Therefore,

I believe and know that you can control the BEAR of addiction. Either we have free will, or we do not.

Let us look at a man tormented for many years by demons, but the ten thousand demons inside him could not stop him from worshipping the Lord.

> And they arrived at the country of the Gadarenes, which is over against Galilee. And when he went forth to land, there met him out of the city a certain man, which had devils long time, and ware no clothes, neither abode in any house, but in the tombs. When he saw Jesus, he cried out, and fell down before him, and with a loud voice said, What have I to do with thee, Jesus, thou Son of God most high? I beseech thee, torment me not. (For he had commanded the unclean spirit to come out of the man. For oftentimes it had caught him: and he was kept bound with chains and in fetters; and he brake the bands, and was driven of the devil into the wilderness.) And Jesus asked him, saying, What is thy name? And he said, Legion: because many devils were entered into him. And they besought him that he would not command them to go out into the deep. And there was there an herd of many swine feeding on the mountain: and they besought him that he would suffer them to enter into them. And he suffered them. Then went the devils out of the man, and entered

into the swine: and the herd ran violently down a steep place into the lake, and were choked. When they that fed them saw what was done, they fled, and went and told it in the city and in the country. Then they went out to see what was done; and came to Jesus, and found the man, out of whom the devils were departed, sitting at the feet of Jesus, clothed, and in his right mind: and they were afraid. They also which saw it told them by what means he that was possessed of the devils was healed. Then the whole multitude of the country of the Gadarenes round about besought him to depart from them; for they were taken with great fear: and he went up into the ship, and returned back again. Now the man out of whom the devils were departed besought him that he might be with him: but Jesus sent him away, saying, Return to thine own house, and shew how great things God hath done unto thee. And he went his way, and published throughout the whole city how great things Jesus had done unto him. (Luke 8:26–39) (see also Mark 5:1–20)

I would like to bring out many aspects of this story, but I want to stay focused on the fact that the demons could not stop the Gadarene from coming to the Lord. As a result, the man got his healing. This was not just a BEAR of addiction that the man was fighting. These were actual demons dwelling inside him. Also, notice that the man was found healed, clothed, at the feet of the Lord, and in his right mind. If you want peace of mind and help fighting the BEAR of addiction, you must get to the Lord. Seek and you shall find. Knock, and it shall be opened to you.

Good news lies ahead! There is an addiction mentioned in the scriptures, which is good!

> Let all your things be done with charity. I beseech you, brethren, (ye know the house of Stephanas, that it is the firstfruits of Achaia, and that they have addicted themselves to the ministry of the saints,) That ye submit yourselves unto such, and to every one that helpeth with us, and laboureth. I am glad of the coming of Stephanas and Fortunatus and Achaicus: for that which was lacking on your part they have supplied. For they have refreshed my spirit and yours: therefore acknowledge ye them that are such. (1 Corinthians 16:14–18)

Paul ends his first letter to the Corinthians with a few commendations and advice. He tells them to do everything in love. Then Paul brings up Stephanas. He says Stephanas and his household had addicted themselves to the ministry of the saints. What is the ministry of the saints? This commendation of Paul meant that Stephanas, Fortunatus, and Achaicus went above and beyond what was normal to take care of the needs of their brothers and sisters in the church. They supplied the needs that the Corinthians lacked. Then he got detailed and personal. Paul said they refreshed his spirit and the Corinthians.

Have you ever been around someone who refreshed you? That does not necessarily mean that person gave you a cup of coffee, a place to sit, or a gift. It could mean that just being in their presence and talking to them made you feel better within minutes. There are people out there like this. We should be one of them, addicted to helping the people of God.

Try this prayer: Lord, I come with a BEAR of addiction (*name it. Call it out*). It controls my thoughts. It seems to control everything. I cannot shake it. I must have help to fight this BEAR. (At this point, if you recognize that your dad, mother, grandfather, or grandmother had the same or similar problem, call their name out to the Lord.) Lord, you know (*person's name*) had the same BEAR in his life. I must stop it before it spreads to my children. I know You are faithful and can help me. When the urges come, help me to walk away and pray. I need strength. In the name of Jesus Christ, amen.

REBELLION

"For rebellion is as the sin of witchcraft, and stubbornness is as iniquity and idolatry. Because thou hast rejected the word of the LORD, he hath also rejected thee from being king" (1 Samuel 15:23).

We conclude the LIONs and BEARs with the most deadly of them all—the BEAR of rebellion. The words and actions of this BEAR will stir the anger in God faster than any other. This BEAR is so deadly that it kept a whole nation of people and the man the Lord chose to lead them to miss the Promised Land. It cost Saul, who was handpicked by God as the first king of Israel, his throne. Israel paid the high price of slavery and bondage for generations throughout the Bible because they rebelled.

I am a student of history. If I can learn from those mistakes, I hopefully will not make the same ones. I want to provoke the Lord to bless me through my obedience to His Word and not curse me through my rebellion.

What is rebellion (biblically)? It is the public or private resistance to the Word of God; deliberate disobedience. We set ourselves up for failure whenever we choose not to follow God's Word. The BEAR of rebellion hates authority—more specifically, the Bible. Rebellion will cause us to blame God for things we do not understand. Rebellion will cause us to do something and make us believe we are getting even with God. The BEAR of rebellion begins with the attitude that you can have it your way. Some phrases that the BEAR of rebellion uses are: "That's in the Old Testament," "The Bible is not for us today," and "The Bible is an antiquated book that is not significant in today's society." The BEAR of rebellion is cancerous and must destroy all authority to survive.

God is not a democracy. He is autonomous. He does not exist for our pleasure. We exist for and by His pleasure. We need to understand the concept that God does not need us. We need Him. When the Lord breathed life into Adam, He exhaled. At any time, God has the right to inhale and take it back. After all, it is His breath. Not ours.

Let us learn from Saul and the price he paid for disobeying the Lord.

> And the LORD sent thee on a journey, and said, Go and utterly destroy the sinners the Amalekites, and fight against them until they be consumed. Wherefore then didst thou not obey the voice of the LORD, but didst fly upon the spoil, and didst evil in the sight of the LORD? And Saul said unto Samuel, Yea, I have obeyed the voice of the LORD, and have gone the way which the LORD sent me, and have brought Agag the king of Amalek, and have utterly destroyed the Amalekites. But the people took of the spoil, sheep and oxen, the chief of the things

which should have been utterly destroyed, to sacrifice unto the LORD thy God in Gilgal. And Samuel said, Hath the LORD as great delight in burnt offerings and sacrifices, as in obeying the voice of the LORD? Behold, to obey is better than sacrifice, and to hearken than the fat of rams. For rebellion is as the sin of witchcraft, and stubbornness is as iniquity and idolatry. Because thou hast rejected the word of the LORD, he hath also rejected thee from being king. And Saul said unto Samuel, I have sinned: for I have transgressed the commandment of the LORD, and thy words: because I feared the people, and obeyed their voice. Now therefore, I pray thee, pardon my sin, and turn again with me, that I may worship the LORD. And Samuel said unto Saul, I will not return with thee: for thou hast rejected the word of the LORD, and the LORD hath rejected thee from being king over Israel. (1 Samuel 15:18–26)

The Lord told Saul what to do and how to do it. There was no guesswork on Saul's part, no misunderstanding. Saul's excuse was that he feared the people and listened to them. Here is a little advice: listening to everyone's opinions will cause you a lot of heartaches. If you must have everyone's input on what you should or should not do, you will be miserable. There is nothing wrong with advice, but there is no substitute for obedience to God's word.

Samuel compared rebellion to witchcraft. Why? Witchcraft is a form of idolatry, which is forbidden, according to one of the Ten Commandments: Thou shalt have no other god before me. Research the Bible about witchcraft. It is not pretty, and you will find out quickly He does not like it. If the Lord compares rebellion to witchcraft, I urge you to be diligent in keeping the BEAR of rebellion under lock and key. Then, throw away the key!

For those who think rebellion is an Old Testament subject, the Lord did not change His mind in the New Testament, where we see the longsuffering, mercy, and patience of Jesus Christ. In the Old Testament, we saw judgment. Black and white. No gray areas. Then read the book of Revelation. Judgment is coming, and it will catch many by surprise.

The BEAR of rebellion has been roaring across our land for decades. Policies and agendas are in place that are in direct conflict with the Bible. Again, if an issue is socially correct, there is a good chance it is against the Bible. Just because it is popular does not mean it is right; if it is popular, it is probably *not* right. Have you noticed how so many things are getting worse in our country?

Let's look at Israel in the Old Testament. As long as they were serving and worshipping the Lord, they had plenty and were safe from their enemies. However, when they disobeyed the Lord, started worshipping idols, and listened to the BEAR of rebellion, enemies overtook them. They took their possessions and put them into slavery, sometimes for generations. And they would stay in bondage until someone stood up and said, "We must repent and get back to God."

The BEAR of rebellion is a bully. It will make a lot of

promises that it cannot keep. It is a salesperson who will pull you in and sell you problems that will take you years to get out of, and it will always be someone else's fault that you are in that situation. The BEAR of rebellion is a narcissistic ego trip on steroids, and you are the only one who can control it.

Here are a few ideas for how to keep this BEAR in check:

1. Make up your mind that you will serve the Lord with all your heart, mind, soul, and strength (Joshua 24:15);
2. Work on your humility (2 Chronicles 7:14);
3. Do the right things (Ephesians 5:1–11); and
4. Learn to be obedient (Hebrews 13:7, 17; Isaiah 1:19–20).

Try this prayer: Lord, thank you for loving me enough to expose the LIONs and BEARs in my life. I need help getting my attitude and ego under control. The BEAR of rebellion gets riled up inside me when I hear and see things I do not like or agree with. This BEAR triggers so many emotions that I know can destroy me and those around me. Please give me the strength and wisdom to keep this BEAR under control. In the name of Jesus Christ, amen.

GOLIATHS

But the men that went up with him said, We be not able to go up against the people; for they are stronger than we. And they brought up an evil report of the land which they had searched unto the children of Israel, saying, The land, through which we have gone to search it, is a land that eateth up the inhabitants thereof; and all the people that we saw in it are men of a great stature. And there we saw the giants, the sons of Anak, which come of the giants: and we were in our own sight as grasshoppers, and so we were in their sight.

—NUMBERS 13:31–33

GIANTS

As we begin to understand the GOLIATHs that will appear in our lives, let us remember that they are external sources of conflict that may occur at any time or place without much notice. GOLIATHs are giants. They are loud. They are bullies. They take intimidation to another level. Therefore, we must follow the advice of Peter: "Be sober, be vigilant; because your adversary the devil, as a roaring lion, walketh about, seeking whom he may devour: Whom resist stedfast in the faith, knowing that the same afflictions are accomplished in your brethren that are in the world" (1 Peter 5:8–9).

Keep your spiritual radar operational 24/7. There is nothing that the devil would like to do more than catch you off guard.

A preacher, who we will call Bro. James, was in a dilemma. A little old lady in the church, who we will call Sis. Jones, was a constant thorn in his side. Whatever he was for, she was against it. Whatever he was against, she was for it. Her mission seemed to be very focused in opposing the preacher in every matter.

It got so bad that he contacted a friend and confidant,

who we will call Bro. Tom. Bro. James described the stress and heartache that Sis. Jones had created in the church. It was horrible. The preacher lost sleep and his appetite, and his nerves were almost shot. He told his friend he was ready to throw in the towel and step down as pastor.

Bro. Tom asked Bro. James if any other people in the congregation were like Sis. Jones. He wondered if she had others on her side also working against the preacher.

Bro. James said that it was just her.

Bro. Tom asked for clarification: "Do you mean she is the only person in the congregation giving you a hard time?"

"Yes, she is the only one, but she consistently tries to keep trouble stirred up," said Bro. James.

Bro. Tom, still wanting more understanding, said, "No one is on her side? Everyone is standing beside you?"

Bro. James nodded yes.

As you read this story and begin to see the deeper issue, please understand you cannot fully empathize with this preacher until you have faced a GOLIATH like this. A GOLIATH does not have to be a man nine feet tall, four hundred pounds of muscle, with a voice that sounds like a lion roaring or a growl that sounds like thunder in the distance. A GOLIATH in your life can be a ninety-year-old, four feet nine inches tall, blue-haired lady who weighs a hundred pounds soaking wet and can charm a fish out of the water and into the boat. But in your eyes, she is a giant, and when she speaks, she could make the sheriff lock himself up and throw away the key!

Now back to the preacher, Bro. James and his friend and confidant, Bro. Tom.

The friend advised the preacher to hold on and not let Sis. Jones intimidate him. Bro. Tom said, "You're letting *one* person completely dominate your life and ministry. Don't pay her any attention! Sounds like no one else is!"

Bro. Tom left Bro. James with one last bit of encouragement. He said, "Remember, if you do not stay and overcome Sis. Jones, no matter where you pastor, there will always be another Sis. Jones. She may have another name like Sis. Smith, Sis. Williams, or Sis. Taylor. Or, she might be a Bro. Jones at the next church. If you do not fight and overcome, you will face this *giant* again."

Bro. James was encouraged and told his friend he would stay the course. But, it was short-lived because he resigned the following Sunday.

A few months passed, and Bro. Tom came into contact with an evangelist who also knew Bro. James. The evangelist told Bro. Tom that Bro. James was now pastoring in another state. The evangelist said he had recently been in services with Bro. James but had since resigned from that church.

"*What?*" The friend was shocked. "He hadn't been at that church very long."

The evangelist laughed and said, "Bro. James told me I would see you someday, and you would ask why he resigned from the second church. He said to tell you he found Sis. Jones at that church too!"

So how do you fight these GOLIATHs called giants? First, realize what most all giants use as their main weapon: fear. I need to remind you what Paul told Timothy: "For God hath not given us the spirit of fear; but of power, and of love, and of a sound mind" (2 Timothy 1:7).

Where does fear come from? The devil, and he uses

it to empower the GOLIATHs called giants. Until you learn how to control fear, fear will control you.

Also, be reminded of what John said: "Ye are of God, little children, and have overcome them: because greater is he that is in you than he that is in the world" (1 John 4:4). Learn these scriptures. Commit them to memory *and* use them.

Second, there is another tool that you will need to learn, put into practice, and become proficient in. There is power in this phrase: "Satan, I rebuke you in the name of Jesus Christ." Because the giant is empowered by the devil, call him by name and rebuke him. This is the tactic that the Lord used while He was tempted in the wilderness. It still works today.

You will never run long enough or far enough from your GOLIATHs. Just as the original Goliath bullied the army of Israel, the giants will always be there bullying you, until you take authority over them, stand your ground, and be ready to fight for what God has given you.

OFFENSES

> For it was not an enemy that reproached
> me; then I could have borne it: neither was
> it he that hated me that did magnify himself
> against me; then I would have hid myself
> from him: But it was thou, a man mine equal,
> my guide, and mine acquaintance. We took
> sweet counsel together, and walked unto the
> house of God in company. Let death seize
> upon them, and let them go down quick into
> hell: for wickedness is in their dwellings, and
> among them. (Psalm 55:12–15)

David said it was not his enemy who tried to stab him in the back. Nor was it someone who lied about him. It was his friend. His confidant. His brother, who worshipped, sang, and prayed beside him. I want you to remember that David was known as a man after God's own heart, but I am also going to translate verse 15 for you into modern language. "I hope they all die and go to hell!"

How could a man handpicked by God make a statement like that? Even more so, why would God allow that to be recorded in the Bible? It is simple, but you might not like it. God does not suppress anything that He wants us to know. David was a human being with human feelings. When you face the GOLIATHs of offenses, you find out more about yourself than you realize, and sometimes others find out more about you than maybe you should expose. Once the words come from your mouth, they cannot be taken back.

When the GOLIATHs of offenses invade your life, your humanity emerges. The offenses stir anger, wrath, strife, contention, and many other emotions and feelings. A person is like a tea bag. The real them comes out when they get into hot water.

Some of the hardest sayings of Jesus Christ and Paul are these: "Ye have heard that it hath been said, Thou shalt love thy neighbor, and hate thine enemy. But I say unto you, Love your enemies, bless them that curse you, do good to them that hate you, and pray for them which despitefully use you, and persecute you" (Matthew 5:43–44).

> Bless them which persecute you: bless, and curse not. Recompense to no man evil for evil. Provide things honest in the sight of all men. Dearly beloved, avenge not yourselves, but rather give place unto wrath: for it is written, Vengeance is mine; I will repay, saith the Lord. Therefore if thine enemy hunger, feed him; if he thirst, give him drink: for in so doing thou shalt heap coals of fire on his head. Be not overcome of evil, but overcome evil with good. (Romans 12:14, 17, 19–21)

One day I was moving something heavy, and it slipped out of my grasp and rolled back the skin on top of my hand. I cleaned and bandaged it. In a few days, it had healed. But after the scab came off, there was a scar. As I type, I look down, see the scar, and relive the whole episode where I was, what I was doing: the slip, the pain, the blood, the cleaning, the bandaging, the bathing without getting it wet, and then waiting for the scab to come off. The scar will be there for the rest of my life; it all comes back when I look at it.

So it is when we have a traumatic event and are faced with the GOLIATHs of offense. We have all met these GOLIATHs, and they have affected each of us in ways that made scars in our lives. It is what they do. They inflict pain and suffering to cause us to want to give in and quit and say and do things that are normal for us. When we do, we will forever be on the run.

However, if we face these GOLIATHs head-on, remembering what the Lord and Paul both admonished us to do, we *will* overcome. The principle is this, and I not only believe it, I know it, because this scripture has been fulfilled in my life several times: "When a man's ways please the LORD, he maketh even his enemies to be at peace with him" (Proverbs 16:7).

I do not know how the Lord does it, but I can surmise the following scenario. "Satan, that is my child you are messing with. Leave my child alone." When the Lord speaks peace, the wind, the waves, and the enemies *have* to cease.

We will have to fight some fights, and lose and win some battles, but everything happens for a reason. This book was written so you understand that every battle, from every source, has a testimony.

I have fought several GOLIATHs in my walk with the Lord. I have cried. I have prayed. I have fasted. I sought the Lord many times, but His answers were usually ones I wanted to avoid hearing. I found out that the lessons I was learning were for my good and eventually for me to share with others. The Lord would soon send people my way for me to advise them of the LIONs, BEARs, and GOLIATHs that we are fighting.

You will have scars, but they are for a testimony. God knew what Job could go through, but Job did not know. God knew that Shadrach, Meshach, and Abednego would make it through the fire, but they did not know. However, notice they had *their minds made up* that God would deliver them no matter what they had to go through.

Are *you* there yet? When you face the GOLIATHs of offenses, when you are hurt, when you leave the battle wounded and scarred, can you still say everything happens for a reason, and the reason is for my testimony? One thing you take with you when you die and also leave behind is your testimony.

Here is how to fight the GOLIATHs of offense. *Rule number one*, remember the scriptures of Jesus Christ and Paul you have read. Commit them to memory. *Rule number two*, kill the root of bitterness.

"Follow peace with all men, and holiness, without which no man shall see the Lord: Looking diligently lest any man fail of the grace of God; lest any root of bitterness springing up trouble you, and thereby many be defiled" (Hebrews 12:14–15).

The root of bitterness almost overtook David. We can hear the pain coming through the words that he said about his friend. "I said in my haste, all men are liars" (Psalm 116:11).

The GOLIATHs called offenses will plant a seed of bitterness in your heart, and it will take root. If you do not kill the root of bitterness, it will become the lack of love LION, consume your heart, and defile your walk with the Lord. To kill the root of bitterness, refer to rule number one above.

LIARS

Who's your daddy?

> Why do ye not understand my speech? even because ye cannot hear my word. Ye are of your father the devil, and the lusts of your father ye will do. He was a murderer from the beginning, and abode not in the truth, because there is no truth in him. When he speaketh a lie, he speaketh of his own: for he is a liar, and the father of it. (John 8:43–44)

Lying is a specific sin that will cause someone to end up in the Lake of Fire. "But the fearful, and unbelieving, and the abominable, and murderers, and whoremongers, and sorcerers, and idolaters, and all liars, shall have their part in the lake which burneth with fire and brimstone: which is the second death" (Revelation 21:8).

The GOLIATHs called liars want to destroy your testimony, and they will do whatever it takes to steal, kill, or destroy it. No one likes to be lied to or lied on. But the GOLIATHs are sly. They can tell a lie so good that it sounds like the truth.

There was a preacher I never got to meet, but I heard his testimonies. His name was Bishop Mark Lawson, and he blazed a trail for The Church of Jesus Christ (non-LDS) in the early to mid1900s. He was a street preacher during part of his ministry.

One day, in a small town, he began preaching on a street corner. Soon he had a large gathering of very attentive people. Soon afterward, a horse and wagon pulled across the street from where Bishop Lawson was preaching. It was apparent that this was a medicine man by the banner hanging on the covered wagon. The medicine man set up his stage and wares and began to speak. He was selling his cure-all in a bottle. It was *exactly* what everyone needed for any ache or pain. It was the end-all, be-all tonic.

Within minutes, the medicine man had attracted a crowd, and several minutes later, everyone left Bishop Lawson to hear the medicine man.

Bishop Lawson sat on the curb and cried. He told the Lord, "I stand here preaching my heart out, and the next thing I know, everyone is gone. Why, Lord?"

He continued to pray with his head down, not realizing the crowd had dispersed around the medicine man's wagon. Then Bishop Lawson heard a voice and looked up. It was the medicine man standing over him.

Seeing Bishop Lawson sad, he looked down and said, "Preacher, do you know what the problem is?"

Bishop Lawson, still hurting, shook his head.

"The problem is, you tell them the truth, and it sounds like a lie. I tell them a lie, and it sounds like the truth."

Remember, people always end up believing what they want to believe no matter what the truth is.

The Bible warns us about the GOLIATHs called liars. The disciples asked the Lord a question in Matthew 24. Here was His reply.

> And as he sat upon the mount of Olives, the disciples came unto him privately, saying, Tell us, when shall these things be? and what shall be the sign of thy coming, and of the end of the world? And Jesus answered and said unto them, Take heed that no man deceive you. (Matthew 24:3–4)

Do not be deceived. These GOLIATHs called liars are abominations according to Proverbs 6:17, 19. These GOLIATHs called liars claim to love God but hate their brothers, according to 1 John 4:20. These GOLIATHs called liars have invaded the church, and many congregations have followed them, according to 2 Timothy 4:3–4.

So how do I fight these GOLIATHs? Stopping them is almost impossible. Even though you cannot stop the liars, you can control yourself from reacting to them and destroying your testimony. Paul gave Timothy and Titus advice on how to stop liars. "Against an elder receive not an accusation, but before two or three witnesses" (1 Timothy 5:19).

"For there are many unruly and vain talkers and deceivers, specially they of the circumcision: Whose mouths must be stopped, who subvert whole houses, teaching things which they ought not, for filthy lucre's sake" (Titus 1:10–11).

When the GOLIATHs called liars make accusations, spread rumors, and start and keep trouble going, your duty is to stop them to the best of your ability, and you stop them with truth. However, if they will not listen to reason, nor repent, and continue lying, Paul gave additional advice to the Romans on how to handle them: "Now I beseech you, brethren, mark them which cause divisions and offences contrary to the doctrine which ye have learned; and avoid them. For they that are such serve not our Lord Jesus Christ, but their own belly; and by good words and fair speeches deceive the hearts of the simple" (Romans 16:17–18).

Paul said to *mark them* and *avoid them*. Paul also classified them as those who are *not* servants of Jesus Christ. Someone might say, "But they are still Christians." No they are not. Christians cannot lie without admitting they're wrong and asking for forgiveness. True repentance will cause a true Christian to make things right. As a result, we find out if someone is a true Christian or, down deep inside, one of the GOLIATHs called liars. The Lord said we would know them by their fruit (actions).

Remember, prevention is an excellent start in handling these GOLIATHs. Mark them. Avoid them. They are *not* your friend. They will tell a lie to tell a lie, and they want to pull you into it. If you hang around these GOLIATHs long enough, you will become a liar too.

INSTIGATORS

There are GOLIATHs called instigators. They are toxic. They are abominations unto the Lord. "An heart that deviseth wicked imaginations, feet that be swift in running to mischief ... and he that soweth discord among brethren" (Proverbs 6:18–19).

Let us take a minute to look at the word *abomination*. The words abomination, abominations, and abominable appear 117 times in the King James Version of the Bible. It would be a great Bible study to see where these scriptures are and what they have to say. Not only do we need to know the things that are pleasing to the Lord and that will bring blessings to us, but we should also take time to find out the things that are detestable to, morally disgusting to, and abhorred by God.

We all know sin is sin. There are no white lies or black lies. However, the Bible names some things the Lord classifies as absolutely despicable. These issues, I believe, are sins that push the envelope of eternal damnation. Revelation 21:8 and Proverbs 6:17 and 19 say that liars are abominations and will have their part in the Lake of Fire. Is it possible that these sins are worse than other sins? I know some theologians are well-versed on sin and understand many concepts that I do not, but for some reason, the Lord saw fit for us to know that some sins stick out to Him more than others. They are called abominations, and the GOLIATHs called instigators are abominations.

Where do these GOLIATHs originate? Instigators come from a diseased heart.

> And GOD saw that the wickedness of man was great in the earth, and that every imagination of the thoughts of his heart was only evil continually. And it repented the LORD that he had made man on the earth, and it grieved him at his heart. And the LORD said, I will destroy man whom I have created from the face of the earth; both man, and beast, and the creeping thing, and the fowls of the air; for it repenteth me that I have made them. But Noah found grace in the eyes of the LORD. (Genesis 6:5–8)

The wickedness of man was so great that even the imaginations of his heart were continuously evil. Are we there again today? There is so much evil and wickedness in high places, as Paul told the Ephesians, that if we knew everything that was going on, we would not be able to sleep tonight. We are so close to the Lord's return! Hallelujah! Even so, come, Lord Jesus!

But Noah found grace in the eyes of the Lord. Does the Lord see something special in you? Are you provoking Him to blessings or judgment? It might be judgment if you are an Instigator.

Here are more words from the Lord through Zechariah.

> These are the things that ye shall do; speak
> ye every man the truth to his neighbor;
> execute the judgment of truth and peace in
> your gates: and let none of you imagine evil
> in your hearts against his neighbor; and love
> no false oath: for all these are things that I
> hate, saith the LORD. (Zechariah 8:16–17)

Can you see where instigators have diseased hearts? Most doctors will tell you that heart disease, if left untreated, will cause many other problems in your body and, ultimately, death. Remember, for everything in the natural realm, something corresponds in the spiritual realm. If you do not take the necessary steps to prevent or treat a spiritually diseased heart, you may become an abomination unto the Lord and experience the second death in the Lake of Fire.

Many have read or heard the passage that says there is none righteous: no, not one. Let us look at the whole passage.

> As it is written, there is none righteous, no,
> not one: There is none that understandeth,
> there is none that seeketh after God. They
> are all gone out of the way, they are together
> become unprofitable; there is none that
> doeth good, no, not one. Their throat is an
> open sepulchre; with their tongues they have
> used deceit; the poison of asps is under
> their lips: Whose mouth is full of cursing and

bitterness: Their feet are swift to shed blood:
Destruction and misery are in their ways:
And the way of peace have they not known:
There is no fear of God before their eyes.
(Romans 3:10–18)

Can you see some of the same verbiage as to what God calls abominations? Can you see the symptoms of spiritually diseased hearts afflicting these people?

The GOLIATHs have to be faced head-on. John had to deal with an Instigator named Diotrephes. Read how John handled him.

I wrote unto the church: but Diotrephes, who loveth to have the preeminence among them, receiveth us not. Wherefore, if I come, I will remember his deeds which he doeth, prating against us with malicious words: and not content therewith, neither doth he himself receive the brethren, and forbiddeth them that would, and casteth them out of the church. (3 John 1:9–10)

John said he would remember his deeds, how he used berating words against him, refusing to receive the brethren and excommunicating anyone that tries to be hospitable to them. Have you ever had friends who wanted to control who your friends were? How their enemies had to be your enemies too? This was Diotrephes. He was a GOLIATH.

Some might say it sounds like John was holding a grudge. Actually, he was far from holding a grudge. John was letting the church know he knew who the instigator was, what the instigator was doing, and that he would face the instigator if he could get there. If you give GOLIATH an inch, he will take a mile. There is also the saying that if you give the devil and inch, he will become a ruler. And so it is with GOLIATHs called instigators.

Here is how to handle potential GOLIATHs called instigators. Do not feed their fire. Mind your own business. When the GOLIATHs called instigators try to get you stirred up, walk away. Remember, they are looking for a reaction from you that they can tell someone else. They may be recording you without your knowledge. Then they will edit the recording to push their agenda. "Where no wood is, there the fire goeth out: so where there is no talebearer, the strife ceaseth. As coals are to burning coals, and wood to fire; so is a contentious man to kindle strife" (Proverbs 26:20).

Some people love drama. If there isn't any drama going on, they will start some. You can see their eyes light up when they get to tell gossip on someone. They are GOLIATHs called instigators and they will pull you in, make you part of the drama, and destroy your testimony. Like the GOLIATHs called liars, *mark them* and *avoid them.*

ACCEPTANCE

"Love not the world, neither the things that are in the world. If any man love the world, the love of the Father is not in him. For all that is in the world, the lust of the flesh, and the lust of the eyes, and the pride of life, is not of the Father, but is of the world. And the world passeth away, and the lust thereof: but he that doeth the will of God abideth for ever" (1 John 2:15–17).

Many people want to be accepted. They want to feel part of something. They want to have a sense of belonging. Social media platforms have proven this fact. One of my favorites (enter sarcasm mode) is, "If you don't 'like' this post and forward it to every one of your friends, then you are ashamed of Jesus," I promise you, your walk with or love for Jesus Christ is *not* based on how many social media posts, friends, or followers you have.

Many people have compromised core beliefs and principles to be accepted by others, and in doing so, the mind games of the GOLIATHs called acceptance have destroyed the walk with God of many people.

Here's the logic. It's popular; therefore, it must be right. It's fashionable; therefore, it must be right. It's socially acceptable; therefore, it must be right. The United States Supreme Court says it's legal; therefore, it must be right. The Constitution of the United States gives me the right; therefore, it must be right. The GOLIATHs called acceptance want you to believe that all these statements are logical, factual, and true. Society has allowed the GOLIATHs called acceptance to take the Word of God, water it down, insert humanistic philosophy, and create a whole new way of thinking that is far from the truth of God's Word. There is only one truth, and that is the Bible. God's Word is infallible.

God neither wants nor needs our opinions, logic, philosophies, or justifications; He wants our obedience. He wants our trust and faith in Him that He is God and God alone. He wants us to accept Him and Him alone, but every time we fall into the traps set by the GOLIATHs of acceptance, we are, in a sense, creating our own god that we will follow.

The problem the children of God find is when the GOLIATHs called acceptance bully us. Acceptance is sneaky, looks for weaknesses of his prey, entices people to do things they would not normally do, and uses mass and social media to push ideologies contrary to God's Word.

The companionship and fellowship of believers in Jesus Christ are not matched in any other organization or entity. The difference is when there are only two or three children of God together focused on getting something done, there is another person there, Jesus Christ, and it usually gets done. You cannot find this guarantee in any other theology. "Again I say unto you, that if two of you shall agree on earth as touching any thing that they shall ask, it shall be done for them of my Father which is in heaven. For where two or three are gathered together in my name, there am I in the midst of them" (Matthew 18:19–20).

Acceptance wants to pull us away from fellowship, especially where Jesus Christ is Involved. That's one foe that the GOLIATHs of acceptance know they cannot beat.

One of the foremost biblical examples of the effects of the GOLIATHs called acceptance is Demas. We also learn about Paul from his letter to Timothy that he was like us and needed companionship and fellowship. Demas had left Paul, and Paul was lonely. Being lonely is a horrible feeling. "Do thy diligence to come shortly unto me: For Demas hath forsaken me, having loved this present world, and is departed unto Thessalonica; Crescens to Galatia, Titus unto Dalmatia. Only Luke is with me. Take Mark, and bring him with thee: for he is profitable to me for the ministry" (2 Timothy 4:9–11).

I need you to hurry, says Paul. It's just Luke and me. Bring Mark too. Then Paul shows how much of an impact Mark is on his life: "For he is profitable to me for the ministry." (see 2 Timothy 4:11) What a wonderful compliment. That connection and fellowship between Paul and Mark was near impervious. Is it possible that Demas once had the same relationship with Paul as Mark? Possibly. I can almost hear the hurt in Paul's tone. Demas had not just left Paul, he had *forsaken* Paul, which is much harsher. They may have had stern words, or Demas may have just left in the middle of the night without notice. We do not know. All we know is that the GOLIATH of acceptance had enticed Demas through the lusts of the flesh and eyes, and the pride of life, which are the weapons the GOLIATHs of acceptance use against God's people.

Paul warned the Church in Corinth about social issues and how they would be affected if they fell into the traps set by the GOLIATHs of acceptance.

> Be ye not unequally yoked together with unbelievers: for what fellowship hath righteousness with unrighteousness? and what communion hath light with darkness? And what concord hath Christ with Belial? or what part hath he that believeth with an infidel? And what agreement hath the temple of God with idols? for ye are the temple of the living God; as God hath said, I will dwell in them, and walk in them; and I will be their God, and they shall be my people. Wherefore come out from among them, and be ye separate, saith the Lord, and touch not the unclean thing; and I will receive you, And will be a Father unto you, and ye shall be my sons and daughters, saith the Lord Almighty. (2 Corinthians 6:14–18)

First, understand the phrase "unequally yoked with unbelievers." We are given the command to go into all the world and preach the Gospel of Jesus Christ. As we do, we must be ever so vigilant of the GOLIATHs of acceptance. These GOLIATHs will tell us that God is love, and we must remind them that God is also a God of judgment. These GOLIATHs will say that if we do not accept and embrace the socially accepted issues of today, we are preaching hate, and we have to remind them that we do not follow society. We are Christians, and Christians follow not only the four gospels; we follow the whole Bible, which is the infallible Word of God.

If we fall into the traps set by the GOLIATHs of acceptance and refuse to repent and change, we will have problems with God. We become "unequally yoked with unbelievers" when we accept or condone their sin. When the Bible says it is sin, it is wrong, and our opinions, logic, philosophy, and justifications are irrelevant in the courtroom of heaven.

Do we need to start calling out everyone's sins? *Yes* and *no*. Before you go calling out others' sins, make sure your house is clean first, and pray for wisdom. Remember, first things first. "Jesus said unto him, Thou shalt love the Lord thy God with all thy heart, and with all thy soul, and with all thy mind. This is the first and great commandment" (Matthew 22:37–38).

Yes, if they first love the Lord with all their heart, mind, soul, and strength and are in a position and frame of mind that showing them their error may bring them closer to the Lord. *No*, because if they do not love the Lord with all their heart, mind, soul, and strength and the time and place are not right, you may tear down more in five minutes than a sincere child of God can build up in five years.

Some use the Word of God like a madman using an axe chopping wood: Wood chips fly everywhere, and people run for safety. Others use the Word of God as skillfully as a surgeon with a scalpel—delicately, tenderly hoping the instrument in his or her hand will bring healing to the sick and diseased. You might be the madman, or you might be the surgeon. I pray that you are or will become skilled in handling God's Word and will lead many to the Lord through wisdom and patience.

Second, there must be a definite difference between the children of God and the world. These were Paul's words, not mine. In coming out from among them and being separate people, we are not to have our noses in the air. Children of God *should not* have egos. Let me say it again. Christians *should not* have egos. The Lord said in John 13:35, "By this shall all men know that ye are my disciples, if ye have love one to another." You had better love someone before you start telling others how wrong they are. In like manner, if you have children, they need to know you love them before you correct them.

Lastly, there are blessings that come with separating ourselves from this world and fighting the GOLIATHs of acceptance. The Lord will receive us, be a Father to us, and call us his sons and daughters. In other words, we will be accepted by Him, He will protect and provide for us as a father does his children, and we will be part of His inheritance. We are either seeking to be accepted by this world and the GOLIATHs of acceptance or by Jesus Christ. Our actions are what make up our testimony and show to whom we give our allegiance.

Remember, he knows you. He knows your weaknesses and what entices you. If you think you do not have any weaknesses or things that tempt you, you are lying to yourself. You are human and will battle some form of weakness and temptation for the rest of your life. Since he knows so much about you, you *must* be on guard. You will also need to assess the things that draw you away from God, and avoid them. The old folks used to have a phrase: "There are some things that you need to get shed of."

The writer in Hebrews said almost the same thing. "Wherefore seeing we also are compassed about with so great a cloud of witnesses, let us lay aside every weight, and the sin which doth so easily beset us, and let us run with patience the race that is set before us" (Hebrews 12:1).

Some weights are not sins, yet they will pull you down and keep you from fully serving the Lord with all your heart, mind, soul, and strength. Then, there are sins. We know sin separates us from God, yet we push God away every time we give in to sin. Until you "get shed" of these weights and sins, you will keep falling into the traps set by the GOLIATH called acceptance.

TASKMASTERS

"Therefore they did set over them taskmasters to afflict them with their burdens. And they built for Pharaoh treasure cities, Pithom and Raamses" (Exodus 1:11).

"Lest Satan should get an advantage of us: for we are not ignorant of his devices" (2 Corinthians 2:11).

Slavery is alive and well today. Its prevalence is not as noticeable since it has been made unlawful by the law of the land, but it still exists covertly.

Another type of slavery that is not discussed but is worldwide and in almost every household is spiritual slavery, and we will now address the GOLIATHs of slavery called taskmasters.

The Hebrews in Egypt were both physical and spiritual slaves. Pharaoh kept them in bondage and made them build the temples and pyramids that we still have today. He also kept them from sacrificing to and worshipping God. The taskmasters' goal was to control every aspect of their lives.

And Pharaoh commanded the same day
the taskmasters of the people, and their

officers, saying, Ye shall no more give the
people straw to make brick, as heretofore:
let them go and gather straw for themselves.
And the tale of the bricks, which they did
make heretofore, ye shall lay upon them;
ye shall not diminish ought thereof: for they
be idle; therefore they cry, saying, Let us
go and sacrifice to our God. Let there more
work be laid upon the men, that they may
labor therein; and let them not regard vain
words. And the taskmasters of the people
went out, and their officers, and they spake
to the people, saying, Thus saith Pharaoh, I
will not give you straw. Go ye, get you straw
where ye can find it: yet not ought of your
work shall be diminished. So the people
were scattered abroad throughout all the
land of Egypt to gather stubble instead of
straw. And the taskmasters hasted them,
saying, Fulfil your works, your daily tasks,
as when there was straw. (Exodus 5:6–13)

Not only did Pharaoh want complete physical control
of the Hebrews, he wanted something that is given to
every person freely, but once spent, you can no longer get
it back: time. Pharaoh wanted the Hebrews' time. Pharaoh
accused the Hebrews of having too much time on their
hands. All they could talk about was going to sacrifice to
their God. So Pharaoh ruled that straw would no longer
be provided to make bricks. The Hebrews had to get the
straw themselves, and their production of bricks could not
be diminished.

We are under the same GOLIATHs called taskmasters today. They are not called Pharaohs, but they are the control of the same devil. One of the greatest assets given to you is time, and the devil wants you to waste your time and not serve the Lord. "Remember now thy Creator in the days of thy youth, while the evil days come not, nor the years draw nigh, when thou shalt say, I have no pleasure in them" (Ecclesiastes 12:1).

"Train up a child in the way he should go: and when he is old, he will not depart from it" (Proverbs 22:6). The devil is not an idiot. He is the ultimate GOLIATH taking on the form of a taskmaster. He understands scripture deeper than you or I ever will in this life. He also understands that if you train a child while he is young, the chances are great that the child will continue with the principles learned at an early age. The principle Solomon gave us in Proverbs 22:6 is true in every way. It works from good and righteous perspectives as well as evil and wicked perspectives.

Many of the "well informed" might say we are supposed to train animals and teach children, but it is only their opinion. We have to judge who is right, them or the Bible. I will stick with the Bible because training and teaching are two different concepts.

When someone enlists in the military, they go to basic *training*, not basic *teaching*. When someone chooses a trade or career, they not only have to be taught, they have to be trained. If you take the training aspect out of raising children, they become entitled and lazy. They know the principles, but their teacher did not train them in the application of the principles. They only can tell you what a textbook says or how principles should be taught. They cannot show you how to do it. Therefore, we must train our children in the ways of God, in the things that make Him happy and the things that stir His wrath. The GOLIATHs called taskmasters also know this principle and start training your children to serve them at birth. They take every opportunity you will afford them. These taskmasters love when you let the television become their babysitter. They are ecstatic that they get to entertain them when you give them a cell phone or tablet. All the while you are distracted and thinking they are learning their ABCs and 123s, the GOLIATHs called taskmasters are training our children with commercials, popups, innuendos, and the acceptance of things that are against God. As Paul tells the Corinthians, we should not be ignorant of his devices. They are more subtle than most understand.

If you are not careful, the GOLIATHs called taskmasters also become thieves. "The thief cometh not, but for to steal, and to kill, and to destroy: I am come that they might have life, and that they might have it more abundantly" (John 10:10).

The GOLIATHs called taskmasters enslave people one principle at a time. So slow and subtle are they that it is too late before most people realize what has happened. They are thieves who control a person's heart and mind completely. Would you like to guess what their goal is? If you said, "My soul," you are right. If the taskmasters cannot steal (a type of voluntary control) your blessing or walk with God, they will do their best to kill it (a type of slavery by force). Still, if they cannot steal or kill your blessing or walk with God, the taskmasters will do their best to destroy it (a type of total destruction: "If I can't have you, no one can").

From the beginning, the devil sought to destroy God's

image. He could not destroy God, so his tactics changed to destroy the very creation made in God's image, mankind. "Now the serpent was more subtil than any beast of the field which the LORD God had made. And he said unto the woman, Yea, hath God said, Ye shall not eat of every tree of the garden?" (Genesis 3:1).

God told Adam not to eat the fruit, but He did not tell Eve. Adam had to tell Eve. The serpent knew that to get to Adam, he must get to Eve first because Adam, knowing the word of the Lord, could not be deceived. Therefore, he beguiled Eve first and then let Eve work on Adam. Eve was tricked, but Adam ate the fruit, knowing judgment was coming.

Today, we have deliverance from the GOLIATHs called taskmasters who wants to steal, kill, and destroy. The Lord said He has come so we can have life and have it more abundantly. So are you living or existing? Without Jesus Christ in your life, you are only existing and not living a life of freedom that only He can give. Would the GOLIATHs called taskmasters die for you? Absolutely *not*! Jesus Christ did, but the taskmasters will give you every excuse to stay right where you are. Remember, Jesus Christ gives you the freedom of choice. The GOLIATHs called taskmasters can only enslave you.

If you serve Jesus Christ, have you truly cut all ties with the taskmasters? Are you still sinning? Then, as the Lord said, you are a servant to sin. But why? Some people say we all have to sin a little every day. That sounds like something the GOLIATHs called taskmasters would say, something right out of the devil's playbook and definitely not out of the Bible! If your pastor/preacher says everybody sins a little every day, I have one word for you: *run!* Get away from him or her as fast as you can. This person is a hireling who only cares about income, status, and making everybody happy. This *is not* a person of God.

I understand and have said I have not seen anyone walking on water lately. I know we are human, make mistakes, and sometimes sin, but we are commanded to repent. To say we all sin daily is closely related to an excuse to do and say what we want without repercussions. Biblically, there will be judgment for those who do not repent. The GOLIATHs called taskmasters say you don't have to repent, that God knows your heart. The taskmasters will laugh at you on judgment day because they were able to control your heart and mind.

There are those today who are under the rule of natural taskmasters. Their bosses, spouses, children, or friends want to control their lives. The bosses always want more dedication to the job. The spouses and children can never be pleased, so they must work longer and harder to provide the materialistic things of life that only bring short-term satisfaction. Their friends control who they can be friends with, and their enemies must be mutual. In other words, they say, you cannot be a friend with someone who is my enemy. If you do, then we cannot be friends. The taskmasters exist to control you and keep you in debt and ultimately enslaved.

How do I fight the GOLIATHs called taskmasters? It is time to make a choice. You will either serve Jesus Christ with all your heart, mind, soul, and strength, or you will serve the GOLIATHs called taskmasters. That is a choice only you can make. "Let your moderation be known unto all men. The Lord is at hand" (Philippians 4:5).

If you do not set some boundaries with those trying

Jim Ennis

to control you, you will be under the taskmasters' rule for the rest of your life. No one can fight this battle for you. It is yours, but God helps those who help themselves. Stand up. Speak up. And rebuke the GOLIATHs called taskmasters.

You must say, "You are *not* going to control me and my family because I will take the same stand that Joshua took": "And if it seem evil unto you to serve the LORD, choose you this day whom ye will serve; whether the gods which your fathers served that were on the other side of the flood, or the gods of the Amorites, in whose land ye dwell: but as for me and my house, we will serve the LORD" (Joshua 24:15).

HINDRANCES

"Ye did run well; who did hinder you that ye should not obey the truth?" (Galatians 5:7).

"But he that shall endure unto the end, the same shall be saved" (Matthew 24:13). The GOLIATHs called hindrances come in all shapes and sizes. Just as all GOLITATHs are giants, essentially all GOLIATHs are hindrances. Hindrances are personal and quite real, but we can overcome them. We must understand where the GOLIATHs called hindrances originate if we will be successful in fighting them.

"Wherefore we would have come unto you, even I, Paul, once and again; but Satan hindered us" (1 Thessalonians 2:18). GOLIATHs called hindrances come from Satan. He is the author of confusion and every situation that will cause you to stray from the will and blessings of the Lord.

Now that we know where the GOLIATHs called hindrances come from, let us learn from several scenarios the Bible gives us about how others handled hindrances.

> Then said he unto me, fear not, Daniel: for
> from the first day that thou didst set thine

> heart to understand, and to chasten thyself before thy God, thy words were heard, and I am come for thy words. But the prince of the kingdom of Persia withstood me one and twenty days: but, lo, Michael, one of the chief princes, came to help me; and I remained there with the kings of Persia. (Daniel 10:12–13)

An angel of the Lord came to minister unto Daniel during a trying time. He told Daniel that God heard his prayers from the first day Daniel decided to serve the Lord. Please realize that not all prayers are heard. Just as a parent gets tired of hearing a child who whines, so does the Lord get tired of hearing us always saying "I want" or "I need."

First and foremost, we should start our prayers with thanksgiving. Praise will get the Lord's attention every time, but if you only talk to Him when you want or need something, do not be surprised if He starts turning a deaf ear to you. He has no obligation to hear or answer your prayers.

On a side note, James has given us a recipe for the type of prayers that get answered: "The effectual fervent prayer of a righteous man availeth much" (James 5:16). Notice that Daniel set his heart to understand and chastened himself before God. He got his heart right. If your heart is not right, you are wasting your time. Your heart is the beginning of your walk with God because you must first love Him with all your heart (Deuteronomy 6:5; Matthew 22:37–38; Mark 12:30). If your heart is diseased from sin, no worries; God is a great surgeon who will give you a new heart. He can take out that old, diseased heart and create a new heart full of love for Him, and His surgery technique will not leave a scar. All you have to do is ask, start changing your ways (quit listening to the GOLIATHs called hindrances), and do the things that please Him, and He will hear your prayers.

"If my people, which are called by my name, shall humble themselves, and pray, and seek my face, and turn from their wicked ways; then will I hear from heaven, and will forgive their sin, and will heal their land" (2 Chronicles 7:14).

Oops! Did I say change? Yep. Sure did. Daniel chastened himself, and we must do the same. The GOLIATHs called hindrances start causing us problems when we decide to make changes. It is one thing to get your heart fixed, but if you do not change your habits, you will end up right back in the shape you were in before the heart transplant. Ask any cardiovascular doctor. The same principle in the flesh also works in the spirit. You can accept Jesus Christ as your personal Savior, give your heart to God, shake the preacher's hand, be baptized, and join the church, but your prayers will be hindered if you do not change your habits. Consider your ways and quit falling for the traps set by the GOLIATHs called hindrances.

Now therefore thus saith the LORD of hosts; Consider your ways. Ye have sown much, and bring in little; ye eat, but ye have not enough; ye drink, but ye are not filled with drink; ye clothe you, but there is none warm; and he that earneth wages earneth wages

to put it into a bag with holes. Thus saith the
LORD of hosts; Consider your ways. (Haggai
1:5–7)

Stop periodically and assess your walk with Jesus Christ. You may be dealing with a condition known as *Spiritual insanity*. GOLIATHs called hindrances love to entrap you in Spiritual insanity. Spiritual insanity happens when people continue to live the same life with the same old habits and expect God to continue blessing them. There must be change in us. Consider your ways if your prayers are being hindered. Understand that when you get your heart right and change your old habits, He will hear your prayers.

Second, consider that the angel said the prince of the kingdom of Persia withstood him for twenty-one days. Our time is not God's time, and He will answer in His time and manner. It may not be the answer we want, but when we get our hearts right, change our ways, and quit listening to the GOLIATHs called hindrances, we will ask for His will and find contentment in it.

Our next example is the story of Nehemiah and the Jews building a wall around a city.

But it came to pass, that when Sanballat
heard that we builded the wall, he was
wroth, and took great indignation, and
mocked the Jews. And he spake before
his brethren and the army of Samaria,
and said, What do these feeble Jews? will
they fortify themselves? will they sacrifice?
will they make an end in a day? will they

revive the stones out of the heaps of the rubbish which are burned? Now Tobiah the Ammonite was by him, and he said, Even that which they build, if a fox go up, he shall even break down their stone wall. Hear, O our God; for we are despised: and turn their reproach upon their own head, and give them for a prey in the land of captivity: And cover not their iniquity, and let not their sin be blotted out from before thee: for they have provoked thee to anger before the builders. So built we the wall; and all the wall was joined together unto the half thereof: for the people had a mind to work. But it came to pass, that when Sanballat, and Tobiah, and the Arabians, and the Ammonites, and the Ashdodites, heard that the walls of Jerusalem were made up, and that the breaches began to be stopped, then they were very wroth, And conspired all of them together to come and to fight against Jerusalem, and to hinder it. Nevertheless we made our prayer unto our God, and set a watch against them day and night, because of them. (Nehemiah 4:1–9)

Sanballat was incensed that the Jews were building the wall. GOLIATHs called hindrances started running their mouths. Insult after insult, they looked for ways to hinder through chaos. No matter how personal it gets, hindrances, by all means necessary, are there to stop you and the work the Lord has given you to do.

Hindrances also like to travel in packs, just as Tobiah was there to support Sanballat. The devil also understands the principles the Lord gave us: where two or three are gathered in His name or touching anything, He is in the midst, and our prayers will be accomplished. If one does not do the job of hindering, the devil will send two or more. Whatever it takes to hinder, the devil will keep sending the GOLIATHs called hindrances to stop the work of the Lord.

Then Nehemiah started to pray, which is a lesson within itself. Prayer is our most powerful tool in fighting the GOLIATHs called hindrances. Pray. Pray. Pray. Get God involved. Petition the throne for help in your fight.

Like Daniel, they had their hearts and minds made up, and they built the wall because the people had a mind to work. In other words, they had their minds made up that the GOLIATHs called hindrances *would not* stop their work. Even though you have your heart and mind right, it does not mean the GOLIATH called hindrances will give up. Because of your determination, he will step up his game too. The greater the asset you become to God, the more intense the devil has to ramp up his tactics. Just like Sanballat and Tobiah were used by the devil, he will fight you with more people, hoping you cannot take the pressure. More hindrances equal more pressure to give up the fight. *Be aware!* Sometimes the most harmful hindrances will come from the people you love.

What did Nehemiah and the people do? They did what we should do to overcome the GOLIATHs called hindrances. They watched and prayed day and night. The Lord told the disciples the same thing in the garden of

Gethsemane, and He gave the reason why: "Watch and pray, that ye enter not into temptation: the spirit indeed is willing, but the flesh is weak" (Matthew 26:41).

When you need something from the Lord, you will pray more than once and for more than five minutes. If needed, you will pray all night long and ask others to pray with you.

> And it came to pass, when our enemies heard that it was known unto us, and God had brought their counsel to nought, that we returned all of us to the wall, every one unto his work. And it came to pass from that time forth, that the half of my servants wrought in the work, and the other half of them held both the spears, the shields, and the bows, and the habergeons; and the rulers were behind all the house of Judah. They which builded on the wall, and they that bare burdens, with those that laded, every one with one of his hands wrought in the work, and with the other hand held a weapon. (Nehemiah 4:15–17)

Before addressing the next issue, I need to describe your value to the Lord and your threat to the devil. If you have successfully battled the LIONs, BEARs, and GOLIATHs, you are a greater asset to the Lord and a greater threat to the devil. A private in the military is not as valuable an asset as a general. The general has time, experience, and education under his or her belt. A general is a wealth of wisdom and information. The longer you serve the Lord and the more battles you go through and overcome, your wisdom, knowledge, and understanding of spiritual warfare should grow.

Because of your time and experience, you also become a greater threat to the devil. You know *too* much! The devil and his demons have painted a bullseye on your back. They assign every GOLIATH to take you out at all costs. You are known in hell, and a WANTED poster has your picture on it. However, listen to this promise from Paul: "If God be for us, who can be against us?" (Romans 8:31).

Before becoming a general, you must go through basic training, fight some battles, and do your time coming up through the ranks. You must earn your rank and the respect of the troops in order to be a good leader. You cannot demand respect of your brothers and sisters in the Lord just because you are a child of God. Nor will you be an asset to the Lord or a threat to the devil or any of his GOLIATHs just because you demand respect. You are just full of hot air. Humble yourself, pray, fast, study, and ask for the Lord to send you a general (pastor) you can follow. Then watch Him exalt you in His time.

Nehemiah records that the enemies discovered he and the Jews received word about their plans and that God stopped them. Then they went back to work. If you are faithful to the Lord, He will help you fight your battles. He will help you overcome the GOLIATHs called hindrances.

Notice how intense the desire was to build the wall. There was a line of soldiers protecting the workers. Thank God for prayer warriors on the line every day! Thank God for those people in constant contact with the heavenly headquarters! Thank God for people who do not just read a prayer, but when they pray, heaven stands at attention for an incoming message from the front! If you know someone like this, you know the hair on your neck stands up when he or she begins to pray. If you do not know someone who prays like this, ask the Lord to let you experience it and also make you a prayer warrior.

After the soldiers on the line of defense were the workers. The workers worked with one hand and had a weapon in the other. Absolutely no GOLIATH was going to penetrate their ranks. Nothing will stop the work of the Lord, and that is what the Lord said also. "Upon this rock I will build my church; and the gates of hell shall not prevail against it" (Matthew 16:18).

Get into the Church of Jesus Christ and stay. There is safety inside His promise!

Finally, one of the biggest GOLIATHs called hindrances can be found in the home. The original institution ordained by God is the team of husband and wife, and like with Adam and Eve, the devil wants to hinder the husband and wife. The devil knows a divided house cannot stand.

> Likewise, ye wives, be in subjection to your own husbands; that, if any obey not the word, they also may without the word be won by the conversation of the wives; While they behold your chaste conversation coupled with fear. Likewise, ye husbands, dwell with them according to knowledge, giving honor unto the wife, as unto the weaker vessel, and as being heirs together of the grace of life; that your prayers be not hindered. (1 Peter 3:1–2, 7)

If you are a feminist, you probably will not like this section. Feminism is a hindrance simply because the tenets of feminism and the Bible clash. God is *always* right, and everything else is just an opinion. GOLIATHs called hindrances fight against anything that is scriptural.

Peter starts the third chapter in his first book by saying wives need to be subject to their husbands, and through this process, the wives might win their unbelieving husbands to the Lord. No one in his or her right mind can justify being obedient to a husband who is an abuser, mentally or physically. God never intended for the home to be a battleground but a place of refuge from the world, a well of love in a world of hate, and an oasis of refreshing from the toils and struggles of life.

Then Peter speaks to the husbands. A godly husband will live with his wife. He does not just occupy the same house but lives (becomes one) with her. He knows that husbands ought to love their own wives as their own bodies; he who loves his wife loves himself (Ephesians 5:28). The godly husband understands the essential unity God has established between husband and wife. He will also honor his godly wife as the weaker vessel, not the dumber vessel. A wife who will not be in subjection to her godly husband and a husband who will not honor his godly wife cannot be blessed because their prayers will be hindered. The power of a praying and loving husband and wife is a power that the GOLIATHs called hindrances will use every resource available to them to stop. The goal of the GOLIATHs called hindrances is to divide and conquer the husband and wife team and then, ultimately the home. Again, they know the power of a praying and loving husband and wife, and that power must be broken at all costs.

Finally, the GOLIATHs called hindrances are numerous. They usually come into your life in small ways, but remember, they are GOLIATHs and will continually grow if you allow them. Stop them when they are small. Pray for wisdom and to be alerted when your paths cross with the GOLIATHs called hindrances.

CONCLUSION
(BUT NOT REALLY)

I pray that you now recognize the LIONs and BEARS that you face and battle in your everyday life. We *must* face them, fight them, and overcome them before we can effectively battle the GOLIATHs that *will* eventually cross our paths. The LIONs, BEARs, and GOLIATHs are very real and determined to destroy us.

However, the LIONs, BEARs, and GOLIATHs are not the whole story, and we must consider something that many people will forget. Remember that when David went to fight Goliath, he left the sheep behind that had been entrusted to his care.

With the Lord's help, in our next book, we will look at the LAMBs that God has entrusted to our care. Do not get so involved in the battles that you forget the blessings that have been given to you and charged to your care.

Until then, maintain your integrity, walk with the Lord, and never, ever give in.